Be Happy

35 POWERFUL METHODS FOR PERSONAL GROWTH & WELL-BEING

Dr. Rebecca Ray

FOUNDER OF THE
HAPPI HABITS PROGRAM

Brimming with creative inspiration, how-to projects, and useful information to enrich your everyday life, Quarto Knows is a favorite destination for those pursuing their interests and passions. Visit our site and dig deeper with our books into your area of interest: Quarto Creates, Quarto Cooks, Quarto Homes, Quarto Lives, Quarto Drives, Quarto Explores, Quarto Gifts, or Quarto Kids.

Text © 2018 by Dr. Rebecca Ray
Art © Shutterstock

This edition published in 2020 by Crestline,
an imprint of The Quarto Group
142 West 36th Street, 4th Floor
New York, NY 10018 USA
T (212) 779-4972 F (212) 779-6058
www.QuartoKnows.com

First published in 2018 by Rock Point, an imprint of The Quarto Group,
142 West 36th Street, 4th Floor, New York, NY 10018, USA

Crestline titles are also available at discount for retail, wholesale, promotional, and bulk purchase. For details, contact the Special Sales Manager by email at specialsales@quarto.com or by mail at The Quarto Group, Attn: Special Sales Manager, 100 Cummings Center Suite 265D, Beverly, MA 01915, USA.

10 9 8 7 6 5 4 3 2 1

ISBN: 978-0-7858-3812-8

Editorial Director: Rage Kindelsperger
Creative Director: Merideth Harte
Designer: Merideth Harte and Jen Cogliantry
Managing Editor: Erin Canning
Editorial Project Manager: Chris Krovatin

Printed in China TT062020

This book provides general information on forming positive habits. It does not provide any medical information regarding mental or emotional health. The author and publisher are in no way responsible for any actions of behaviors undertaken by the reader of this book.

Dedication

To every single one of my clients, for sharing yourselves with me.
To Rage and all at Quarto, for making this a reality.
To Clare and Ben, for saying yes after one phone call.
To Alexis, for being on the other side of the ocean.
And to Nyssa, for being everything.

CONTENTS

INTRODUCTION

This book is in your hands for a reason. Maybe it's because you refuse to settle for a mediocre form of happiness. Maybe you are thirsty for techniques that can boost your daily well-being. Maybe you could do with a moment to yourself to work on your quality of life, rather than caring for someone else all the time. Or maybe you received this book from someone who cares about you.

However it ended up in your possession, this book invites you into the global conversation on happiness and how we can create more of it. Here, I've collected all of the strategies that I've found most effective for boosting your sense of happiness and well-being. These strategies are based on a combination of the science behind happiness and my clinical experience in walking alongside clients on their journeys to becoming happier people. Now, it's your turn. Come walk with us.

HOW TO USE THIS BOOK

You've probably already figured out that this book is about fostering habits for happiness. But before we move on, I want to clarify what I mean by happiness, just to make sure we're speaking the same language.

Happiness itself is an emotional state, and as emotional states go, it's fickle and impermanent, especially when you want it most. In *Be Happy*, I'm talking about the broader concept of well-being, the one that includes all the ingredients we need to feel an overall sense of happiness.

I like to use Martin Seligman's theory of flourishing, which includes the following components:

A) Positive emotions;

B) Activities that provide a sense of engagement (or flow);

C) Healthy relationships;

D) A sense of meaning and purpose; and

E) A sense of accomplishment.

From this list alone, you can see that it's not as simple as just becoming happy and then holding onto that pleasant emotional state with a white-knuckled grip.

The good news is that you have a great deal of control over these happiness ingredients, and in this book, I'll appeal to your inner control freak and show you just how to take your ability to thrive into your own hands. But before I lull you into a false sense of security, we should talk about the aspects of your own happiness that are not within your control.

HOW TO USE THIS BOOK

Sonja Lyubomirsky's happiness pie chart divides the contributing factors to happiness into pieces. First, you can't control your genetics. Thanks to the magic of your conception and birth (it does happen by magic, doesn't it?), you have a predetermined set point for happiness. The combination of your personality and your genetic makeup account for 50 percent of your happiness. Second (and here's the kicker), the things we think will contribute to our happiness don't actually do much for our overall well-being. The vacation house with the private beach, the sports car you've always dreamed of owning—these things contribute to a measly 10 percent of your happiness. On top of that, any new possession or positive change in your circumstances (e.g., a pay raise) only changes happiness in the short term because of how adaptive we are as human beings. You can win the lotto and, thanks to a process called "hedonic adaptation," end up just as happy (or unhappy) as you were before your bank account swelled, because you adapted to your new circumstances.

The good news is that the final piece of the happiness pie is large and controllable. That's right: you control at least 40 percent of your own happiness through your own choices and actions. This book will show you exactly which actions are going to shift you from simply surviving to all-out thriving.

Here's the thing: I've always been a fan of "fast"—not necessarily in the quick-fix kind of way, but in a this-fits-easily-into-my-day kind of way. And that's exactly what this book aims to do: provide you with a set of tools that you can access on your own terms, in your own time.

Read this book from cover to cover, or open this book to the section you need, depending on what you're facing today—it's up to you. The book is divided into four sections: Choosing, Cultivating, Practicing, and Making Space For, with each of these sections diving into areas of our personal power. We have power in:

CHOOSING emotional states and values that help us to live full lives based on what's important to us deep down.

CULTIVATING habits and routines that provide the architecture for a life of flourishing.

PRACTICING (over and over again) methods that create a well-being mindset.

MAKING SPACE FOR life when it gets hard, so you can face the many ways life trips you up without getting stuck.

At the end of each chapter, you'll find a sidebar titled **Make A Habit of . . .** This is where we put these lessons to work and look at ways we can cement positivity into our everyday lives. After taking time to look inward while reading these chapters and identifying which parts of your life you'd like to change, use these closing sections to focus your energy toward making an actual difference.

Congratulations on acknowledging that you can get more out of life. The habits to come will show you how. Let's go!

CHOOSING . . .

joy
gratitude
kindness
patience
laughter
the bright side
courage
self-love
flow

Happiness is a transient emotional state—it can be hard to find, and harder still to hold onto for long. Some days, it may disappear for no good reason at all and leave you scrambling for other emotions to fill its place. Luckily, thriving is a psychological state that doesn't just rely on positive feelings like happiness, but on the daily choices we make. Want to live a rich, vital, fulfilling life? Choose your focus. Choose your actions.

While reading this first chapter, take some time to reflect on the choices you are currently making versus the choices described here. Sometimes our choices are unconscious, and it's not until we are presented with alternatives that we realize we've been sabotaging ourselves all along.

So, let's talk about the daily choices that determine (a) the emotional states we want to embody, and (b) the personal values we can connect with along the way.

CHOOSING ... joy

"Find out where joy resides, and give it a voice far beyond singing. For to miss the joy is to miss all."
—ROBERT LOUIS STEVENSON

We are blessed with the capacity to feel all the "colors" of the emotional rainbow, but too often we miss the brightest one. Joy, like all strong feelings, brings us closer to our true selves.

Before you worry that I'm going to sermonize about "just being positive," I promise you I am not, would not, will never. I know it's not that simple, and so do you. Our brains are problem-solving machines, designed to identify threats and keep us safe. They are not designed to revel in the bounty of tiny happy things that make the world beautiful. It's easy for the small joys to slip out of our grasp quickly, or pass by unnoticed altogether.

Our innate brain wiring is why we're unable to focus on positive things all the time. But we don't have to remain fixed in a negative emotional state because of that. We can deepen our experience of joy by focusing on the things that bring delight into our lives when they occur. A cool breeze on warm skin. An unexpected phone call from your best friend. A warm interaction with a stranger on the train. It doesn't matter what the situation is, and it doesn't matter what "brand" of joy it is— delight, elation, contentment, bliss, gladness. What matters is that we stop to notice it, embrace it, and celebrate it.

What I'm saying is that we can choose joy by savoring it. Joy is magnified when we savor the things that make us happy, no matter how small or large those things may be. But savoring requires you to be present. You need to be connected to the moment to drink it in, not stuck in the past or worried about the future (no easy feat, I know). Research has shown that we benefit from directly experiencing a moment as it is without viewing it through all the past experiences, memories, beliefs, and judgments that we carry through our lives. By mindfully savoring positive experiences, we can prolong and intensify positive feelings—and who doesn't want that?

Choosing Joy

Savor positive experiences by doing the following.

SHOWING YOUR JOY

Smile, pump your fist, do a backflip (somewhere that offers a soft landing!), shake your rump . . . whatever does it for you, take a moment to express your joy. Don't keep it inside—what good is it to you there?

CELEBRATING YOUR JOY

Whether it's your happy moment or someone else's, take time to celebrate it. The celebration could be a simple hug or a card with some encouraging words, or it could be a party for a hundred of your closest friends! The point is that unless you make an occasion of things that are worth celebrating, they will generally pass you by—along with their significance in the progress of your life.

TALKING ABOUT YOUR JOY

When someone asks you how you are, or how your day was, remember to talk about the little happy things. The compliment you received on your outfit, the encouragement you received from your boss on this month's sales figures—these things count as part of the fabric of your life. They give it color. And if you don't celebrate the color when it's there, you run the risk of only seeing gray.

REMEMBERING YOUR JOY

If you're facing a difficult time, you have the choice to remember times when you felt better than you are feeling now. Keep a Joy List handy—a list of events, moments, and experiences that make you smile when you remember them. Draw from this list when you need a dose of delight in your day.

CHOOSING . . . gratitude

> "When I started counting my blessings,
> my whole life turned around."
> —WILLIE NELSON

If I were asked to name the most life-altering tool for ongoing happiness, it would be choosing to focus on gratitude. We live in a culture that constantly sends us messages of "not enough," selling us on the idea that we need more to be happy—more possessions, more money, more friends, more likes on social media. For all of the conveniences that the Internet gives us, it also gives us countless avenues for feelings of inadequacy by making us constantly compare ourselves to others whom we believe to be happier than we are because they only posted the good moments from their vacation.

Gratitude does the opposite: It puts us at peace with what is. It allows us to revel in what we already have by not overlooking it for something shinier in the distance. In other words, gratitude is the birthplace of enough, and enough is the birthplace of contentment.

Let's be real here: being in a state of "not enough" is automatic for most of us now. But the way out of the disease is in front of you, beside you, and within you.

Life with a gratitude habit helps counteract negative feelings such as jealousy, resentment, and entitlement. Holding a deep appreciation for where we are on our journey, the people around us, and the things we've collected along the way helps us shift from stressed to calm, from self-focused to other-focused, and from pessimism to optimism.

So, how do we choose gratitude? We choose it with intention, with diligence, and with acceptance that it won't always change our moments in the short term, but it will transform our lives in the long run.

MAKE A HABIT OF . . .

Choosing Gratitude

Here are three ways to cement gratitude into your life.

GRATITUDE JOURNALING

Record three things for which you are grateful each day in a journal. Writing about an experience makes it more profound and has great emotional benefits. Focus not just on the big, obvious good things, but also on the small, incidental things that strike a chord with you. And most of all, don't forget to focus on the people around you, and the kindness you receive from them.

GRATITUDE CONVERSATION

Resist the urge to lament about the day's problems all night. Instead, once you've vented about your day, share a conversation about what you're thankful for. Take turns sharing your thanks out loud. Shared gratitude magnifies in intensity and strengthens your relationships.

GRATITUDE JAR

Make notes of the things you are grateful for on small pieces of brightly colored paper. Fold each piece of paper and place it in a jar. This jar will become a fountain of gratitude when you need a reminder of what there is to be thankful for in your world. Now you have a tangible record for you to reflect upon.

CHOOSING . . . kindness

"It really shocks me when I encounter people who think kindness doesn't matter. Because I think it's pretty much the only thing that matters."
—JOSH RADNOR

I choose to believe in kindness because I think it's the most important choice we can make in a world that gives us so many excuses to be cruel. I believe in kindness for the greater good, but also for the way it fortifies our relationships with others, from the people closest to our hearts to members of our communities we'll never meet. Choosing kindness is choosing connectedness.

I don't need to remind you that kindness is a surefire way to feel good. Doing something for someone else, especially if it takes some effort on your behalf, is action for happiness—both yours and theirs. Share the love and it's not just others who will benefit, it's the person doing the love sharing too. Kind people feel happier. And this only continues the cycle: Increase your happiness and you're likely to be kinder too.

Kindness holds hands with gratitude. One encourages the other. When we are consciously grateful for the kindness bestowed on us by someone else, it sparks a pay-it-forward cycle.

On days when you're not feeling all that sunny emotionally, start with gratitude. Gratitude is the grounding force that will remind you of what's good (no matter how small) and lift you up so that you're able to pass that goodness onto others. Not being kind is difficult when you're already feeling grateful.

Feel grateful for kindness.   **Pass it on.**   Feel happy that you were kind.

I should mention here that kindness to others is important, but it's almost impossible to be authentically kind to others if you are being unkind to yourself. You count. Acting like you don't is not moving you any closer to happiness. Be mindful of the way you speak to yourself, the time you give yourself to enjoy life, and the amount of time you rest and recuperate. Self-kindness will only increase your kindness towards others and will lead you to go out into the world with a softer, more open approach. Keep your eyes open and you'll see no shortage of opportunities for kindness that the world is offering you.

Choosing Kindness

Here are some ways to spread kindness throughout your life.

RANDOM ACTS OF KINDNESS
Sometimes, the most powerful acts of kindness are the ones that no one knows about except the recipient, who may or may not know you as the source. Buy a homeless person a meal. Donate to your favorite charity. Pay for the coffee of the person behind you in line at Starbucks. Help an elderly person to the car with their groceries.

KINDNESS TO YOUR LOVED ONES
Loved ones are easy to take for granted. Start being more conscious of how you can make a difference to those people who make a difference to you just by being in your life. Write to a friend you haven't heard from in a while. Put your phone down and really listen to your partner when you ask

about their day. Babysit for your brother. Pick your mother-in-law up from the airport.

KINDNESS TO YOURSELF
I'm not just talking about making every day a "treat yourself" day, okay? Yes, those days are good, too, but kindness happens internally as much as externally. Speak kindly to yourself. Use encouraging words. Give yourself time to rest. Remind yourself of how well you are doing. Remind yourself to keep going. Remind yourself you are worthy.

CHOOSING ... patience

> "The key to everything is patience.
> You get the chicken by hatching the egg,
> not by smashing it."
> —ARNOLD H. GLASOW

As someone with a bachelor's degree in Impatience, I'm not here to wag my finger and preach to you about how patience is a virtue. It's just that I can't speak about happiness unless I cover those things that I know to be the most important contributors to happiness, even when those things require a significant degree of effort. You have to be patient with patience.

I'm the first to get easily swept up in the speed of life. As I said earlier, I'm a fan of fast. I have a tendency to decide what I want to do or where I want to go and then wanting to be there instantaneously. On my good days, I might accept a minimum amount of effort before I lapse back into impatient desires to be there/be done/have arrived.

So, what? Buying into the need to hustle to get happier, make your dreams come true, find love, or get to work on time feeds into the fear system in our brains. It feeds the idea of scarcity and convinces us that there's not enough of everything to go around. It feeds the idea that rest is only for the weak. And the urgency this creates is a trigger for surviving, but not for thriving. When we are in survival mode, our bodies are flooded with stress hormones such as cortisol and adrenaline—

hormones that cloud our creativity, tangle our thoughts, and convince us that we have very few options for solving the problems sitting in front of us.

I'm not saying you shouldn't work hard. I'm saying that working hard in a lifestyle that also includes rest, play, and reasonable time for the general demands of daily life will nourish your mind, heart, and soul so much more than "rise and grind" ever will.

But how do we do this in a culture that warns us that we risk our very worth as humans if we stop to catch our breath? (Side note: I'm not saying that as a fact; I'm simply repeating the messages we receive on a daily basis from the media.) The answer is tough but necessary: We choose patience. We choose to step back, to take full and complete breaths, and to reject the idea that things don't get done unless we rush at and through them. We choose patience for the times we don't get it right and the times obstacles show up. And we choose to forgive ourselves when we default to rushing because we buy into keeping up with the crowd and fitting in.

Patience is a mindset as much as it is an emotional state. It's a value and a way of being. It's important to note that you can work hard and choose patience. You can follow your dreams and choose patience. You can be healing and patient. And you can be patient in all the roles you fulfill daily: partner, parent, child, sibling, friend, colleague, teammate, grandparent.

MAKE A HABIT OF . . .

Choosing Patience

Here are some ways to remain patient in an impatient world.

GIVE UP THE RUSH

Become aware of racing thoughts and racing actions. Make a choice to give up the rush for a period of time. Start with small choices, such as driving more carefully on the way to work. Perhaps you will give yourself one day in the week that you commit to single-tasking and not trying to do a million things at once.

LOSE TIME

Get radical! For one day, take your watch off and keep your phone in your pocket. You don't have to check the time every five minutes to know what you need to do next.

HAVE FAITH

Trust that life is happening as it needs to right now. Trust yourself to do what you need to do in order to create the life you want to live, without compromising your well-being in the process. Rushing things won't make you happier, but you'll certainly be happy when things happen and you're already thriving by the time they do.

CHOOSING . . . laughter

> "Life is worth living as long as
> there's a laugh in it."
> —L. M. MONTGOMERY, *ANNE OF GREEN GABLES*

The relationship between humor and happiness is fundamental. Being able to see the funny side of life helps us cope when life doesn't go our way. It helps us to manage the relentless problem-solving machines that are our brains by interjecting reasons to not take life all that seriously. Yes, we are wired to focus on everything that has gone wrong and will go wrong. What we are less likely to do is to find a way to see the positive, even ridiculous, side to difficult situations.

In my work as a psychologist, I often see how protective humor is. I see it enable people to keep doing their jobs in situations that can only be described as horrendous. I see it help people heal. I see it help people talk through their problems by scaffolding the discussion with humor to prevent things from getting too emotionally heavy too quickly. Humor is the light in our lives. It interrupts the shadows of our problems, even just momentarily, to brings us back into the light.

However, choosing humor is not about laughing inappropriately in the face of pain. It's not about invalidating what's hurt you or laughing at another person's experience in a way that hurts or invalidates her. Choosing humor is about being able to step into a different perspective when it's possible and appropriate (that is, you can laugh at anything in the privacy of your own head, just be careful at what comes out of your mouth, okay?). Choosing humor is about changing the default lens through which we usually see life.

When you choose humor, you automatically experience an increase in pleasant feelings. But that doesn't mean that you have to be a comedian about every part of your life. No, it means that you can find the playful side of yourself, the side that can razz and banter, rib and gag. It's about the choice you have to give up the business side of life for a minute and remember that you don't need permission to have fun.

And if you needed another reason to look on the funny side, humor is a bonding agent. It brings us closer together. You know that person who gets you? You probably feel that way because they laugh at the same things you do. You share the same humor dialect. And when things get tough, that person is often just as medicinal as any other alternative you have available. Side note: We usually have people in our lives that play different roles. We need the person who listens to the pain and gives a piece of sage advice as much as we need the person who makes us laugh until our bellies hurt. Sometimes this might be the same person, sometimes not. Be open to your friends and their strengths. They will shine at different times and for different reasons.

Choosing Laughter

Below are some ways to laugh when you feel like yelling.

LOOK FOR LAUGHTER

When confronted with a tough situation, ask yourself the following questions:

1. Is there a funny side to this?

2. Will I look back on this and laugh? Can I laugh at it now?

3. Who could show me the funny side?

FUNNY JOURNAL

Grab your journal and pen and record three funny incidents or moments from your day. Writing them down helps to prolong the positive feelings and makes us conscious of the small, hilarious things that may otherwise pass by unnoticed.

FUNNY TRIBE

Find the people who make you laugh and keep them with you. Keep them close, seek them out, love them hard. They are the ones who will help you see the lighter side when you can't do so for yourself.

CHOOSING . . . the bright side

"Optimists are right. So are pessimists. It's up to you to choose which you will be."
—HARVEY MACKAY

If there is any topic on which your inherent choice needs to be emphasized, it is choosing to look on the optimistic side of events rather than on the pessimistic side. It's true that our brains have a bias towards negativity, thanks to the pesky need to focus on survival that we inherited from our ancestors. This means that it's natural to focus on problems. It's natural for our minds to first point out the things that aren't working, or our flaws and mistakes, or the obstacles in front of our goals.

What's not usually automatic is looking towards the brighter side of how things might work out.

Your sense of happiness and contentment will grow when you focus your energies on things turning out for the better (perhaps not always the best, but for the better) in the long run. And when things go wrong, optimism strengthens your capacity to be able to cope, recover, and rebuild.

Whether your viewpoint is optimistic or pessimistic depends on three ways you interpret negative events:

A) Do you tend to assume that horrible circumstances or feelings are here to stay, or do you remind yourself that they will pass and give way to better days?

B) Do you tend to view negative things as all-encompassing, as taking up your entire life and defining your entire character, or are you able to view those things in balance with the positive things/characteristics that are also present?

C) Do you take negative things personally and turn the blame upon yourself, or do you attribute negative things to factors outside of yourself?

The direction in which you interpret negative and positive events has a considerable impact on your approach to life overall. Being able to turn toward the bright side of life by choice, and with full acknowledgment that there is effort involved, helps us to move towards thriving. It's a choice we make, even when our typical state might be to focus on the negative. Our default states can even change over time, if we take the time to practice new ways of thinking that eventually rewire our brains.

Why would you bother, though? If it's difficult to do, why would you add the extra effort to your life when you might already be struggling to simply get through the day? Because healthy well-being is a project that takes an entire lifetime, and because you're here trying to improve yourself. A choice toward optimism is a choice towards your future happiness.

Choosing the Bright Side

Here's how to make a habit of staying positive.

LOOK ON THE BRIGHTER SIDE

Ask yourself the following questions:

1. Is there a positive side here?

2. Will I look back on this and see that there is a bright side? Can I see that side now?

3. Who could show me the bright side?

IMAGINING THE GOOD

Grab your journal and pen and pick an area of your life that is a priority for you right now. It might be your role as a parent, it might be your business, or perhaps it's your health. Take at least ten minutes to journal about this area of your life working out exactly as you dreamed it would be. If everything went your way, and dreams came true, what would it look like? Allow yourself to shift into your hope and feel what it's like to imagine the good. Do this for as many life areas as need them.

REFLECTING ON WHEN THINGS HAVE TURNED OUT WELL

Take a moment to look back on times when you entered into a negative place. (I know, it hurts. But trust me, there's a reason for it.) Now think of how things actually turned out. Was it as bad as you thought it would be? And if it was bad at the time, what did it bring into your life that was ultimately good for your well-being? A special person? A new perspective? A lesson learned?

CHOOSING . . . courage

"Courage starts with showing up
and letting ourselves be seen."
—BRENÉ BROWN

You don't have to go far to find an inspirational quote on courage accompanied by the requisite picture of a majestic lion or a guy with a barrel chest standing on top of a mountain. It's a frame of mind that has been packaged so much that we sometimes need a reminder that scrolling by a quote on courage in your Instagram feed and sharing it because you wholeheartedly agree with it is not the same thing as taking a courageous action.

Caveat: I'm not saying that you need to be climbing mountains, or even "doing one thing every day that scares you" (unless that's your jam, of course). What I'm saying is that living courageously requires us to do something. It is just as much about the quiet, unseen decisions that we make daily as it is about confronting the bigger goals we set throughout our lives.

You see, courage is not present when life is easy. It doesn't have to be. We don't need courage to go to the store to get some milk, or get ready for work, or vacuum the floor (motivation, yes, but not courage). And we don't need courage to hear positive feedback about how we're doing, or to take stock of our lives when everything seems to be in its place.

We need courage when things get hard. When we want to give up but need to keep going. We need courage when we fail or make a mistake. And when life delivers us a set of circumstances we did not order during our last online shopping spree.

There's a common misconception that courage occurs independently in its own right. It doesn't. Courage doesn't show up unless you need it. So, if you keep yourself safe from emotional discomfort, wrapped up and warm until courage appears so that you may go ahead and truly start living, you may be waiting a very long time and find that you are stuck before you've even started.

You see, courage is right there beside you when fear is loudest, rejection is nipping at your heels, and shame is ready to parade you naked to the world. Courage shows up when we know the risks but we do it anyway. When we say to ourselves that living authentically is more important than staying comfortable. That's where you'll find courage. And courage is contagious.

So, you know that thing you have to give to the world? Please put it out there. Please take the step and trust that courage will show up. Doing so is the only way that we live fully, richly and deeply, and doing so is the greatest gift you can give yourself and the people around you. Choose to live with courage and authenticity, because that's true beauty.

Choosing Courage

Want to take courageous action when the going gets tough? These tips might help.

ACCEPT DISCOMFORT

Lean into the discomfort. Accept that fear will show up. Accept that in order to find your courage, you have to first face the fear. And then commit to taking it with you by allowing it to have a seat on the bus next to all your other emotions. Just know that you're still in the driver's seat.

GET CLARITY ON WHY

Unless you're clear on why you need/want to do the thing that is demanding courage from you, it will be much harder to move forward. Know your *Why* and courage has a reason to join you. Know your *Why* and it will put your fears into perspective. Perhaps your *Why* is because you need to heal. Perhaps it's because someone needs you even when you don't think you're ready.

Or perhaps it's because life has disrupted your plans and you don't know how you'll face tomorrow, let alone where you're headed next. Courage will show you, as long as you remember what kind of person you are trying to be.

DO IT, AND THEN DO IT AGAIN (OR DO THE NEXT COURAGEOUS THING)

Like confidence, courage is built like an emotional muscle. Use it again and again and your comfort zone becomes wider, richer. The more you use it, the quicker courage arrives. It's not that you no longer feel fear—you will. But you'll no longer listen to it like it's the director of your life.

CHOOSING . . . self-love

*"You have been criticizing yourself for years,
and it hasn't worked. Try approving of
yourself and see what happens."*
—LOUISE L. HAY

Perhaps your Internal Board of Criticism is already holding a meeting about the title of this section. Perhaps its members are already warning you that self-love is simply some gimmick for the Soft Ones and that the only thing you need is to be reminded of your faults and all the ways that you don't measure up to help you stay on the straight and narrow.

I don't buy it. And I hope, by now, that you don't either. Because I will put money on the fact that you, my dear friend, have had years of practice listening to your Internal Board of Criticism. And where has it gotten you? Has it ever actually helped?

I'll bet not. I'll bet that, instead, the scolding and reprimanding that those inner voices have tossed your way have only served to keep you stuck in patterns of self-sabotage, of procrastination, of I'll-do-it-someday and only-when-I'm-good-enough. I'll also bet that those voices are so automatic by now that you don't always know when they are speaking, or at the very best, you listen to them because you are convinced that it's in your best interest to do so, because it will make you a better version of whatever it is that you're trying to be.

That's nonsense. There is no amount of self-criticism that I've ever seen help someone on their way to better well-being. And just so we're clear: I'm not talking about admitting when you've made a mistake and resolving to do better next time. I'm talking about the chatter that constantly tells you that you are not the right dress size or weight, or pretty enough, or smart enough, or important enough, or rich enough, or good enough on any level. These are the voices that tell you you're a bad mother, son, sister, friend, employee, business owner, or person in general.

And I get it: You don't choose these voices. These voices are just there. But you have another option and that is to choose self-love. To choose to reform your relationship with yourself. To start treating yourself like you are worthy, valuable, and worth taking care of.

As I said earlier, it's not easy to overcome default thought or behavior patterns. But with conscious awareness, you can befriend yourself—and then watch as your well-being, productivity, confidence, and general happiness bloom!

Choosing Self-Love

Here are some tips for fostering everyday self-love.

QUIT THE HABIT OF HATING YOURSELF

Ask yourself the following:

1. Would you speak to a friend like this?

2. Would you treat a friend like this?

3. If you acted like this towards a friend, would that person feel good about themselves?

4. If you acted like this toward a friend, would they be motivated to move forward with their life?

RESPECT YOUR NEEDS

Check in with your needs and respect them.
Need encouragement? Give it.
Need rest? Take it.
Need exercise? Do it.
Need nutritious food? Eat it.
Do what needs to be done to respect yourself.

ACKNOWLEDGE YOUR STRENGTHS

When was the last time you acknowledged your personal strengths? When was the last time you spoke aloud the things you like about yourself? Make a list of those things and read it—every day, if you need to—until it becomes ingrained. Can't think of anything right now? Get someone close to you who you trust to help you make that list. Take it seriously—treat this list like it is your own personal charter.

CHOOSING ... flow

"It is by being fully involved with every detail of our lives, whether good or bad, that we find happiness— not by trying to look for it directly."
—MIHALY CSIKSZENTMIHALYI

Flow is that pleasant state of being so completely absorbed in an activity that you lose your sense of time. It's the mental state characterized by sharpened focus for an activity that brings you into the "zone"—the place where you are engrossed in what you are doing in an enjoyable, motivational way.

I have an ambivalent relationship with flow. Don't get me wrong: I adore this state. But, by nature, I don't love effort of any kind, and the idea that I have to put in effort to get to flow makes me wonder whether or not it's really worth it. Writing is my gateway to flow, but it's rare for me to be excited about the effort of sitting down and plugging away in order to be there when flow comes over me. And I never know how long that might take. It could be within five minutes, or it could be an hour later. What I do know is that unless I show up in the first place, flow won't find me.

When was the last time you did something that absorbed your attention to the point of losing time? To the point that you were so engaged in the activity that you experienced your world in macro view, zooming in on just your space, your moment, your thing?

Flow is a feeding tube to happiness. Do more things that help you access this mental state and you'll nourish your well-being. Often the problem is that we don't give ourselves the time to do the things that invite flow. And often, it's the initial effort that we are quick to reject, with excuses of "can't be bothered" or "do it later." And before we know it, we are caught up in doing too many of the have-to activities and not enough of the want-to activities.

For you, it might be a creative pursuit, such as painting or playing music. Perhaps it's rock climbing, running, reading, or planning your next home renovation. Whatever it is, the activity is about what it brings you. It's an interaction of mindful effort with the reward of the activity itself.

Please be aware that if it's an activity like social media scrolling or phone gaming, it might not be the flow you're looking for. These activities can at times be cathartic and entertaining, but they can quickly become an absorption that is out of balance with the other aspects of your life. When I refer to flow here, I'm talking about the activities that add to your well-being, rather than ones that deaden your awareness because of their addictive qualities, which cause you to ignore other areas of your life.

Choosing Flow

Put your flow first with these habits.

GET MINDFUL

Start small: Commit to five minutes of your chosen activity in which you focus solely on that activity. And then do exactly what mindfulness masters do: when your attention wanders, gently bring it back to the task. Mindfulness and flow are two sides of the same coin—one leads to the other and back again.

GET CURIOUS

What if you don't recognize the activities that get you into a state of flow? Get curious about this. Start a research campaign in your own life, looking at what you do that engages you completely and pleases you infinitely. And if you're at a point in your life where you aren't doing anything like that for yourself, think back to a time when you were. What were those activities? When did you do them? What did they look like?

MAKE TIME

Hands up if you're good at self-sabotage via procrastination, fear of failing, or perfectionism. Hands up if you feel too guilty to make time to do the things that you enjoy. I get it. There are a million other daily responsibilities to take your attention. But if you're serious about your well-being, you need to get serious about prioritizing yourself, and that includes the activities that you want to do, even when they require a bit of effort initially. The longer you remain convinced that you can't possibly find an open space in your calendar to give yourself a chance to find some flow, the more you miss out. And if you're making time but not truly using that time effectively (because you're thinking about doing it but not really doing it, or you show up at that time and then decide to do something else), then flow will escape you. You deserve it. But you have to give it to yourself.

CULTIVATING . . .

your inner life
your rest & sleep
your relationships
your positive feelings
a calm environment
green time
your vision
your values
your goals

The psychological seeds that we plant for well-being determine how we grow across mind, body, and spirit. If you want a flourishing garden, you can't simply plant a few seeds and hope for the best. The same can be said for our health. If we don't continue taking care of our lives and ourselves on an ongoing basis, we can't expect to thrive. The habits you cultivate are fundamental—pick good ones!

But hey, if it were that easy, everyone would be doing it, wouldn't they? But it's not easy, not for any of us. That's why I prefer to talk about habits we can cultivate in short periods of time rather than making a huge transformation in every area of your life at once. This is about doing enough small things to make a big difference to your happiness.

For each new habit discussed in this section, I suggest that you start by giving it a bite-sized amount of attention—say, fifteen minutes per day—and nurturing it consistently. These small actions will build up over time, and before you know it, a positive habit will have taken root.

CULTIVATING . . .
your inner life

"You need to learn how to select your thoughts
just the same way you select your clothes every day.
This is a power you can cultivate."
—ELIZABETH GILBERT

Consider your relationship with your mind:

How does it speak to you?
How do you respond to it?
Do you treat it as if it always tells you the truth?
Does it treat you as if you are a treasured friend?

The reason I ask is because the biggest cause of unhappiness is how we respond to our mental chatter. Generally, it's this relationship that has the strongest influence on our feelings, and therefore, on our emotional well-being as a whole. Your mind feeds your thoughts, memories, self-judgments, and worries, and you buy into them as if they are factual, because this is you you're talking to. This wouldn't be a problem for our happiness if the majority of our thoughts were lovely and positive—but that's just not the case when we are wired for problem-solving.

Our minds explain our world using language that is biased negatively toward things that are threatening, an impulse left over from our caveman days. Our mental software hasn't been updated in a long time. And because of this problem-solving software, it's impossible to control every thought that comes to you. Don't believe me? Just watch. Okay, this is probably not the time to simply quote "Uptown Funk" lyrics to you, but try this: For the next fifteen seconds, don't think about a pink elephant. See? Either you just uncontrollably thought of something, or it took considerable effort not to. It's impossible to simply ignore all your negative thoughts, and ignoring even some of them takes hard work, if it's actually possible at all.

On the flip side, we often act as if our minds have a remote control for our behavior. How many times have you been determined to exercise the following morning, and then woken up and given in to your mind's assertions that it's too cold, or you're too tired, or you'll do it tomorrow, as if your body were controlled by your thoughts? Let's test this. Wherever you're sitting reading this book right now, introduce the thought, "I can't raise my right arm." As you're having that thought, lift your right arm. Now, think of how strongly your mind had you convinced of certain things that you couldn't do. What if you'd told yourself these things were attainable instead? Maybe you would have continued your studies. Maybe you would have started the business you've been dreaming about. Maybe you would have developed the habit of exercising each morning.

The most liberating news I can give you is that you are not your mind. You are not the negative or self-limiting chatter that plays in the background of your head. In the same way that your left calf muscle does not hold the key to your identity, your mind is a part of you, but it's not you. You are the part of you that can step back from yourself and observe your mind and your body. You are bigger than all the parts of you together. Rather than letting your mind be the boss of you, I'm suggesting that you turn your relationship around so that you can get your power back.

By power, I'm talking about control. If you're nodding your head right now, the control freak in me salutes the control freak in you. I get it! And I wish that, when it came to thoughts and feelings, I could give you an ancient key or passcode that would grant you access to your emotional world exactly as you want to experience it today. But we both know I can't do that (sorry). You can't control your mind any more than you can control your feelings. It's just not as simple as "think positive," no matter how many memes on Facebook tell you so. If it were, we would all be happy, all the time.

You might not be able to control the thoughts that come to you, but you can control how you respond to those thoughts. Instead of interpreting them as fact, you can choose to step back from them, detach from them, and separate yourself from them. For thoughts that are not helping you move in the direction of living well (whatever that means to you in the present moment), I suggest not giving them your precious energy. Acknowledge that you will have thoughts that are unhelpful—harmful, even—but they don't need to direct your day, even though you may not be able to make them disappear.

Cultivating Your Inner Life

Let's say there's a thought that you just can't shake, and it's ruining your inner life, and, by extension, your chances at happiness. Use the following process to deal with this negativity.

1. Notice the thoughts. Acknowledge your mind for doing its job to protect you. Now, ask yourself:

- Is the thought helpful right now?
- Have you heard this story from your mind before?
- How old is this story?
- What would happen if you let yourself get all caught up in this story?
- Would it be a good use of your time and energy to pay attention to this thought?

2. Step back from the thought and remember that the thought is not in control. Your mind can say whatever it wants to and you can do the complete opposite, because you get to control your actions.

3. Take action and try to live by these values. Repeat the process as necessary.

CULTIVATING . . .
your rest & sleep

"Almost everything will work again if you
unplug it for a few minutes, including you."
—ANNE LAMOTT

I could go on a rant here about how our lives have never
been more automated than they are now, and yet we spend
less time resting and sleeping than ever, but I'd prefer to
focus on what we can do about it. How did we get it so wrong
for our well-being? I thought these advancements were meant
to make our lives more restful. But the loss of sleep—true,
recharging sleep—is a huge and sadly common factor in
daily unhappiness.

Perhaps you intuitively know why it's a problem because
you've felt it. Maybe you know the wired-but-tired feeling;
the device addiction; the inability to be still; the constant but
mindless connection to the world through a screen. But maybe
you don't know exactly why it's a problem for our brains. Maybe
you just know it because you don't rest or sleep in a way that is
good for you.

Let's talk about why this inability to switch off hurts us.
First, if you can't switch off, you're not going to sleep easily.
And if you're not going to sleep easily, or solidly, then the
consequences are disastrous for your body in terms of energy
and strength, and for your mind in terms of concentration, focus,

and motivation. But there are other concerning consequences that show up, too.

The brain houses a little structure called the hippocampus. In fact, there are two of them, one on either side of the brain; together they are known as the hippocampi. The hippocampus is responsible for helping us process the details of our experiences, and it does this while we sleep. It is an emotional washing machine of sorts, rinsing through our daily experiences and consolidating the details that have captured our attention into long-term memory. Deep sleep recharges our bodies and rapid eye movement sleep (REM sleep, or dream sleep) recharges our psyches. We need both. If you are not getting the right quality or quantity of sleep to reach these phases often enough throughout the night, then the brain can't do its job of consolidation. Ultimately, you will suffer physically and emotionally.

Before our friends who are shift workers or new moms feel overwhelmed with panic please know that your sleep doesn't have to be perfect every night in order for you to enjoy positive well-being. Our brains and bodies are resilient. But the more often you can have a good night's sleep, the better. If you're in a phase of your life in which your sleep is not so great, becoming overwhelmed by it will only worsen your stress levels. Instead, focus on cultivating those sleep habits that help you get quality sleep when you can.

Just as important as sleep itself is the rest we give ourselves—perhaps not every day, but certainly every week. In Western society, we've reached a frenetic pace of activity for activity's sake. We reward and promote busy-ness. "Hustling 24/7" is celebrated without an equally loud acknowledgment that ignoring the fundamental need for rest is damaging for our collective health.

By rest, I mean a mental and physical break. I mean stepping away from screens, from 24/7 connection, and allowing yourself to find stillness. To be absorbed in something enjoyable. To find quiet. What I don't mean by rest is mindlessly scrolling through your preferred social media feed while you attempt to watch a movie or play with your two-year-old at the park. I also don't mean drinking, binge-watching TV, playing phone games, or any other activity that you use for the purposes of "numbing out." This is not switching off, and all it leaves you with is a mood lower than when you started, because the neurons in your brain continue to fire excitedly due to constant stimulation. That's the opposite of what we're going for here.

Without regular, proper rest, we remain psychologically and physically alert, and there is nothing efficient about remaining in this state for cultivating sleep and the restoration of our essential well-being systems. Please see your doctor for advice if your sleep is chronically poor over a long period of time.

Cultivating Your Rest & Sleep

Quality sleep can be yours! Here are a few tips on how to regularly recharge.

GET RESTED

Determine the difference between what truly relaxes you and what numbs you. Activities that numb you are usually activities you do to avoid some kind of pain. Replace them with moments of stillness, which will allow your mind to come back to its center.

GIVE YOURSELF PERMISSION TO REST

Be kind to yourself! It's easy to think of the need for rest as being a weakness and to consider resting as giving in to a biological imperative rather than an essential part of healthy functioning. Make time and space for rest in your schedule (and then do it, no excuses!). Nothing functions well with a dead battery.

PREPARE FOR GOOD SLEEP

Remove or turn off your devices (cell phone, television, tablet, etc.) an hour before bed. Develop a routine that supports you going to sleep and getting up at the same time each day. If you're not asleep within thirty minutes, get up and do something that will tire you rather than stimulate you. Don't stay in bed tossing and turning. Listen to relaxing music to help you get off to sleep (whatever kind that may be— for all I know, you find death metal very calming). Make sure your room is dark and cool, and your bed is comfortable.

CULTIVATING . . .
your relationships

"A career is wonderful, but you
can't curl up with it on a cold night."
—MARILYN MONROE

Loneliness results from a lack of meaningful relationships to draw upon—the type of relationships that feel safe, loving, secure, free of being judged, and generally understood. They might be with your biological family, or with those friends you consider family because of the significant role they play in your life. You might have found them in childhood. At school or college. At tennis on Tuesdays, or drama class, or meditation group. It doesn't matter, because what's important is that you've got them.

Without at least one solid social connection, we suffer. Loneliness is malignant for well-being. We need to connect, not necessarily face-to-face (although it helps) but however we can facilitate it. We need to feel like someone is there for us. Lonely humans experience the world as more overbearing, more overwhelming, and more painful than people who have loved ones to act as a buffer between themselves and the rough parts of life.

Sometimes we lose these connections through no fault of our own. People move away and we lose touch. We grow out of relationships and they come to their natural end, and perhaps we don't yet have a replacement. Family and friends pass away. The cycle of life brings people to us while others move on. And other times, we may play a role in choosing to intentionally change our social circle upon evolving into a different phase of our lives. Or maybe conflict with someone who has crossed a boundary or irrevocably hurt us may cause a relationship to fall apart. Or we may go through a period where our connections suffer because we simply stop making an effort, for whatever reason.

The point is, connections matter. It matters that we make them, nurture them, draw support from them, and move on to develop new connections as life unfolds.

There are two sides to healthy social connections: giving and receiving. It's not rocket science to realize that clichés like "give-and-take" exist when it comes to human interaction because they are true. Relationships are a tidal exchange, a rise and fall of giving love and receiving love in all its forms, so it's worth reflecting on how we do these things. How do we give, and how do we receive? How do we offer, and how do we ask?

Life may put amazing people in our path, but whether or not they become important people in our lives is largely up to how we nurture this exchange. In the same way that we need to tend to our habits, we need to tend to our relationships. Relationships that are neglected do not survive.

Cultivating Your Relationships

Here are some tips for fostering your relationships with others.

REFLECTIONS

Take a moment to reflect on the following:

- What do your social roles mean to you?
- What does it mean to support someone you care about?
- How would you like to be supported?
- What do you do on a regular basis to tend to your social connections?

MAKING NEW CONNECTIONS

Here are some ways to foster new relationships:

- Go where people are doing things you are interested in.
- Ask questions to get to know some people. What do they enjoy?
- When you meet someone you like, arrange to meet again. Make the effort.

- Be open to each new person as a human who has a story that may strike a chord in your heart.

GIVING

Relationships are a give-and-take. Here's how to reach out:

- Make contact regularly.
- Reach out to those who may need your help.
- Remember small details to show they are in your thoughts.
- Ask questions and truly listen to the answers.

RECEIVING

And here's how to take (just as important as giving):

- Don't expect those close to you to be mind readers, especially if they don't see you often.
- Ask for help. If you don't ask, others may genuinely assume that everything is okay.
- Express gratitude. Maintain the cycle of love and give back.

CULTIVATING . . .
your positive feelings

"Don't water your weeds."
—HARVEY MACKAY

Contrary to what you might see, read, or hear from your friends, family, or favorite company's advertising campaign, positive feelings don't just magically occur, nor are they our default setting. Positive and negative emotions may show up for reasons we understand or for no reason at all. But positive feelings like happiness can be cultivated—it just takes a little effort and intention and a choice to participate. We must show up to the events, activities, and situations in which positive feelings are more likely to occur.

Unfortunately, I don't exactly know what those things are for you. Only you know what makes you feel good, so I can't just throw a universal prescription for happy feelings at everyone. For you, it could be fly-fishing or soy candle making. It could be reading or going out with your friends on a Friday night. Maybe it's taking photos of your baby or going for a long drive with your partner. I don't need to know what it is for you—but you do.

The question is: Do you know what those things are? If you do, then perhaps daily demands have gotten in the way for too long now and you've simply gotten out of the habit of scheduling time for joy and fun. If this is the case, your homework is to reschedule your calendar with you as one of the priorities!

But what if it's been so long since you've given yourself permission to create positive feelings that you've forgotten what to do? Perhaps you've been so preoccupied in other areas of your life that you're experiencing an identity crisis of sorts, in which you've lost touch with the playful part of yourself and don't remember who that person is or how to find her.

If you recognize this in yourself, it's time to get curious. Finding ourselves is not about reaching a psychological destination or a point in time. Sometimes it's about uncovering something in ourselves we didn't previously know, or rediscovering something that we had forgotten. And sometimes it's a realization that something we thought to be true is true no longer. Curiosity is the lens that allows us to learn these things about ourselves. Consider this a research phase. Think back to what you used to do that made you feel good. Experiment and see what those things are for you now. And then do them!

A common question I get asked at this point is, "But what if I don't enjoy it?" It's possible you won't enjoy something you test out, even if you have enjoyed it previously. And it's worth remembering that if you've picked up this book because you have been feeling a little low recently, your mind might attempt to convince you that you won't enjoy anything you try. It might protest loudly against anything unfamiliar to protect you from further emotional discomfort, such as anxiety, disappointment, or frustration. The problem is that if you give up your control to your mind, it will take the keys and the car from you so you can never leave the driveway. You have the option to stay stuck, or to give curiosity a turn and go and test it out. You may very well surprise yourself!

Cultivating Your Positive Feelings

Let's change up the habit-forming format a little bit. For fostering positive thoughts, try the following.

LIST 1

Make a list of the things you used to enjoy but haven't done for a while. They could be anything from solitary activities to team sports. Write down everything you can think of without judging it at this point.

LIST 2

Now, make a list of everything that's not on List #1 that you think you might like to try. Maybe it's something on your bucket list, or something that has been recommended to you by someone who knows you well. Again, don't judge it, just write everything down.

EXPERIMENT

It's time to experiment! Obviously, there's a big difference between thinking about doing something and actually doing it. It's essential that you take action. For anything that makes you feel a little nervous, invite a friend along with you. Take note of how you feel and of any assumptions your mind made that turned out to be incorrect.

LIST 3

Now make a list of the things you have tried and enjoyed. This list is the most important of the three, because it is your portal back to the things you enjoy—and if you already have them written down, then you eliminate the excuse of not knowing what to do when you have time to do it!

CULTIVATING . . .
a calm environment

*"Happiness is a place in between
too little and too much."*
—FINNISH PROVERB

I'm not here to evaluate your personality type via the state of your kitchen or cubicle. But what I will say is that the environments in which you spend the majority of your time count significantly towards your happiness. For most of us, that's home and work, maybe the car too, especially if you have a long commute. And when it comes to the environment around you, I don't want to dictate what you must do. I'm not about to tell you to clean your room. Instead, I want you to be true to yourself while creating awareness for the things that might be making your environment more stressful without your realizing it.

Which do you prefer: Clutter or minimalism? Everything in its place or just where you left it last? Quiet or noisy? Bright and colorful or neutral? Are you the type of person who seeks out order or the type of person who can't find your right shoe among the jumble of bags and clothes in the corner of your bedroom? Perhaps you're the type of person who loves filling every spare shelf with something to look at. Or the type of person that savors quiet. Or the type of person whose soul is inspired only when you're surrounded by color.

A calm environment means creating a space that, at best, gives you a sense of peace, and at worst, doesn't add to your stress levels if you're having a bad day. That means that if you come home after the worst day of your week, you don't immediately feel worse because the walls are bright red, the things-that-have-no-home pile is growing in front of your eyes, there's nowhere to sit because your spot has been taken over by the dog, and you can't find your book because it's under a load of unfolded laundry. It also means that when you are at work, your workspace encourages clear thinking, creative problem-solving, productivity, and maybe even inspiration.

Environmental choices are also based on self-knowledge. There is no right look, feel, or design to a space other than the one that you feel brings you a sense of peace.

Let's start with home. Is your home your sanctuary, or is there something about it that stresses you out? Do you have space to relax and catch your breath again? Is it organized in a way that works for you, or are you wasting time constantly trying to find things? Is there enough light? Do you add things to the space that bring you peace (music, candles, etc.)?

Now think about your workspace or office. What does your desk look like? How workable is your filing system? Do you have everything you need at your fingertips to work effectively and efficiently? Are there unnecessary distractions? If these spaces are in disarray, you may be inviting stress rather than calm.

How do you feel when you get into your car? Is it a cemetery of dead coffee cups and takeout containers? Does something need fixing that you've been putting off? Are lost paperwork, shoes, or kid's toys hiding somewhere in the trunk or under the seats?

Feeling calm is an emotion and creating calm is a set of actions that we can choose. We can cultivate a calm environment by organizing the environment around us in such a way that it inspires a sense of personal peace. Take steps to arrange your spaces in a way that brings calm to you.

Cultivating a Calm Environment

Creating a calm environment in your everyday life won't happen overnight, so take your time with these steps, and notice the impact of small changes for your happiness.

ASSESS THE ENVIRONMENT

What's working? What's stressing you out? What could be changed if you were to just put in a little bit of time and effort? What are you making excuses about because it simply seems too hard? What would change if you were to enroll other people in helping you?

PRIORITIZE WHAT CAN BE IMPROVED IN THE SHORT TERM

Perhaps it's a 15-minute cleanup each day. Perhaps it's a day of decluttering. Perhaps it's paying someone to detail your car, or staying back late one afternoon to tidy up your desk.

PLAN FOR THE LONG TERM

Some things just can't be changed immediately. The mustard-yellow wall in your lounge room might need to wait until you've saved enough money to repaint it in your favorite shade of eggplant. Nominate the changes you'd like and take any steps toward doing them that you can right now. A step in the right direction is a step all the same, even if you're not there yet.

ACCEPT WHAT CAN'T BE CHANGED (MAKE UP FOR IT)

And then there are the things you can't change at all, either because they are in a space that is not yours to do whatever you want with, or because other people enjoy that aspect of the space whether you like it or not. Make up for it. Add the touches that would make a difference to you.

CULTIVATING . . .
green time

"Amateurs sit and wait for inspiration,
the rest of us just get up and go to work."
—STEPHEN KING

This is not a hack, as such, but I want to show you a way to think about your time that will help you to see where you are robbing yourself of well-being. Think of all the activities and tasks in your week that deplete your battery as "red time". You know an activity depletes your battery if you feel a little tired after doing it, even if you have a sense of satisfaction when it's over (e.g., "That was a busy but productive day!").

Now, think of the activities and tasks in your week that recharge your battery as "green time". These activities nourish your mind, your body, or your spirit (even if you don't always feel like doing them, such as exercise). They could be anything that sparks your inspiration or gives you a sense of meaning. You'll be able to identify them by the fact that you feel invigorated and/or restored after you do them.

I know you're probably already doing the math in your head here. And I also know that your time is very likely dominated by red time, because it is for most of us. Please know that balancing the two equally is not what I'm suggesting. To adult effectively, we need to fulfill our red-time obligations most of the time. However, problems occur when we don't have any green time at all, or when our green time is not effective enough to offset our red-time requirements.

For example, let's say you work for forty hours each week in a job that you consider to be red time. By the end of your working week, your battery is drained. But you spend Saturday going for a run and then heading out to breakfast with the family before catching up with friends. If these activities rate highly enough, there might be enough spirit-nurturing, battery-charging activities in this comparatively small amount of green time to make up for all the red time in your week.

Perfect balance is unrealistic and usually impossible, but finding the activities that recharge you the most is necessary. It's up to you to figure out whether you have scheduled the right quantity and quality of green time.

Cultivating Green Time

Make sure you have enough green time in your week by doing the following.

LIST 1: RED TIME

Make a list of your red-time activities.

LIST 2: GREEN TIME

Make a list of your green-time activities.

GET COLORING

Pick a week of your schedule and plot it on a calendar, coloring in your red and green times.

ADJUST THE COLOR DISTRIBUTION

Consider what changes you would make if you were treating your mind, body, and spirit according to your best sense of well-being. Remember that we are not going for perfect balance, and there will be some weeks that will naturally be more demanding than others. This is about making sure your green time offsets your red time.

ASK YOURSELF:

- Can you delegate any of your red-time activities to someone else?
- Can you give up any of your red-time activities?
- Can you introduce more green-time activities?
- Do you simply need to give yourself permission to enjoy more green-time activities?

CULTIVATING . . .

your vision

"When I dare to be powerful, to use my strength
in the service of my vision, then it becomes less
and less important whether I am afraid."
—AUDRE LORDE

How will you get to where you are going if you don't know where it is? Where is "there" and what does it look like? You can't expect to be able to live your ideal life if you haven't stopped to consider what that life looks like.

So, what type of life are you trying to create? Where do you see yourself in one year, five years, ten years? These are big questions, so before you get overwhelmed, I'm going to help you break them down. Cultivating the vision you have for your life is about looking at the big picture. It's about getting in touch with your dreams and wishes by letting go of the how and focusing on the why and the what. What does your vision look like, and why is it important for your happiness?

1. BUILDING BLOCKS

Think about the essential elements of your day if you were living the life of your dreams. What would your routine look like? Which habits would you practice? How would you nurture yourself and your relationships? What are the things you'd want to be part of (or not part of) your daily life?

2. BUCKET LIST

Imagine that you're lucky enough to live into your eighties. Now, consider all the experiences you'd like to have in between now and then, from small things to great big dreams. Write that list!

3. BADGES AND BAUBLES

Okay, they might not be things you receive an actual badge for, but in the future you're imagining right now, what are the achievements you want to accomplish, no matter the time frame? And what are the things you'd like to collect along the way? Yes, I know you know that possessions only add 10 percent to our overall happiness, but it's 10 percent all the same. So, it's worth acknowledging the things with which you would like to decorate your life along the way.

Cultivating Your Vision

For cultivating your vision, you're going to have to break out the arts-and-crafts tools.

VISION BOARD

A vision board is a visual representation of the life you dream about. When we get clarity on where we want to head, we have a much better chance of getting *there*; and if not there, then at least in the right direction. A vision board can look however you'd like it to look, but here are some suggestions:

1. Grab a collection of magazines that interest you, scissors, glue, and your journal, or a large piece of cardboard or craft paper.

2. Cut and paste clippings, images, and words across the page that cut to the core of your heart and soul. Or you could cut out pictures and hang them on a string. Get creative. This is your chance to make your mind and heart happy!

3. Hang your collage somewhere you can reflect on it regularly.

CULTIVATING . . . your values

> "It's not hard to make decisions when
> you know what your values are."
> —ROY E. DISNEY

We can't talk about the big picture of your life without also talking about values and goals. For definition purposes, a value underpins a goal. A goal is something you achieve, that has a finite ending. A value is an ongoing set of actions that represents who you want to be.

We are a goal-directed society. We celebrate achieving things, getting runs on the board, winning the game. We often don't stop to consider how we are playing the game, let alone specifically define the set of values that we bring each time we step on the field. But doing so allows us to redefine success in a powerful way.

In your life, what do you want to stand for? What do you want to represent? At the end of your time here on earth, what would you like people to say about you as a person?

To help set the scene, here are some common value words. Circle the ones that you want to embody.

Accepting	Empowered	Passionate
Accomplished	Exciting	Patient
Active	Flexible	Peaceful
Adventurous	Focused	Persistent
Affectionate	Forgiving	Planning
Ambitious	Free	Positive
Assertive	Friendly	Prepared
Authentic	Fun	Present
Autonomous	Generous	Proactive
Beautiful	Goal-oriented	Receptive
Brave	Graceful	Reliable
Calm	Grateful	Resilient
Caring	Grounded	Respectful
Centered	Hard working	Risk-taker
Challenged	Helpful	Self-disciplined
Committed	Honest	Self-respecting
Compassionate	Independent	Self-sufficient
Connected	Indulgent	Silly
Considerate	Influential	Sincere
Consistent	Inspired	Spiritual
Creative	Kind	Spontaneous
Curious	Leader	Strong
Determined	Loving	Successful
Dignified	Loyal	Supportive
Diplomatic	Mindful	Trusting
Direct	Motivated	Vulnerable
Dreamer	Open	Wise
Empathic	Organizing	

Cultivating Your Values

Here's how to cement your values in your everyday life.

1. Grab your journal, your computer, or something in which you can make some notes.

2. Go somewhere that helps you to feel inspired.

3. Consider what's important to you across each major life area. Give yourself a decent amount of time to reflect on the questions below. Write down your answers.

PHYSICAL AND PSYCHOLOGICAL HEALTH

What do you value in terms of your health? Is it important to you to maintain your body and mind?

RELATIONSHIPS

If you were being your ideal self as a partner, son, daughter, parent, sister, brother, friend, and/or colleague, who would you be? How would you act towards those you love?

LEISURE TIME

What values do you have around leisure time? Why does this area of your life deserve your attention?

LEARNING AND PERSONAL GROWTH

What value do you place on ongoing learning and personal growth?

SPIRITUALITY

What value do you place on spirituality? What role does spirituality play in your life? Answer these questions based on what spirituality means for you.

CULTIVATING . . .
your goals

**"It is good to have an end to journey toward;
but it is the journey that matters, in the end."**
—URSULA K. LE GUIN

A sense of accomplishment is a fundamental piece of the puzzle when it comes to our ability to thrive. Goals motivate us. They show us our progress. They help us strive for a better version of ourselves and break through limits that we may have previously thought concrete.

The thing about goals is that it's easy to fail to reach them because we set them ineffectively in the first place. Reaching your goals starts with how well you set the goal at the outset. It's not just about knowing what you want to achieve. It's about being able to distill your endpoint with such clarity that you can then follow steps to arrive at your goal successfully.

How do you do that? With the SMART formula, as explained below.

S – SPECIFIC

You want to get your dream job? Want to get healthy? Want to be a good parent? That's great, but what do these things mean? Be specific about what these goals look like. The more specific you can get with your goal, the clearer the steps will be to get you there.

M – MEANINGFUL

Ensure that the goal is meaningful to you. You won't last long if you are pursuing goals simply to please someone else, based on that person's idea of how your life should be.

A – ADAPTIVE

Make sure that the goal is consistent with your values and designed to take your life in the right direction. Is it going to improve the quality of your life, or are you doing it for reasons that are not consistent with who you are authentically?

R – REALISTIC

I'd like to say you can do anything, but the truth is that working on goals that are too far outside the realm of possibility will demotivate you. I'm not saying that you should lower the bar, only that setting a goal to be an Olympic ice skater when you've never set foot on the ice before might be a tad unrealistic. Don't undersell your potential, but don't start with the unworkable either.

T – TIME-BOUND

If you give yourself unlimited time to complete something, you may never get it done, because there's no reason to do it now. Give yourself an end date as extra motivation to complete your goal.

Cultivating Your Goals

Using the SMART formula, you can make every day goal-oriented.

TRY THE FOLLOWING:

1. Decide what your goal is.

2. Write it up using the SMART formula:
- Specific
- Meaningful
- Adaptive
- Realistic
- Time-bound

3. Start working toward your goal *now*.

4. Review your progress within a week. Consider what's working and what's not working.

5. Revise your goal accordingly and continue working towards your goal with any modifications that need to be made.

6. Once you achieve your goal, celebrate! Savor it.

7. When you're ready, set the next goal.

PRACTICING. . .

mindful productivity

overcoming procrastination

creativity

feeling good enough

forward momentum

breathing

a positive inner voice

setting boundaries

getting perspective

We are constantly evolving, unfolding, and becoming. Allow yourself to be in progress. You don't have to commit to getting "there," because life is not a destination. You need only commit to practicing life as you want to live it each day. Sometimes you'll nail it, sometimes you'll learn. Sometimes you'll throw a tantrum and refuse to do anything, even when you know you're getting in your own way. And sometimes, your own encouraging hand will be the most comforting offer you can extend to yourself.

The point is that happiness is not a finish line that you can cross into a permanent state of bliss. You're only human, and you'll experience the richness of your humanity, good days and bad days included. But as long as you keep practicing, growth will be yours.

PRACTICING . . .

mindful productivity

"You can do two things at once, but you can't focus effectively on two things at once."
—GARY KELLER

How often do you find yourself doing a task but not actually doing it, or doing six things at once but none of them well, or losing focus mid-task and doing anything but what you're supposed to be doing? If this sounds like you, I can relate. Multitasking is seductive, and distraction is fatal when it comes to productivity.

Practicing mindful productivity means harnessing your own self-knowledge to get the best out of yourself. Being mindful means being aware, with an attitude of openness and curiosity. It means training your awareness on whatever it is that requires your focus in the present moment, and gently bringing your attention back to the task when your mind inevitably wanders. Therefore, to be mindfully productive means to focus on one task and to gently refocus whenever your attention wanders, without criticizing yourself because it has.

Remember, this is a practice. Even the most mindful people have days when they are managing their mind as if it were a wayward puppy.

Practicing Mindful Productivity

Here are some ways to practice mindful productivity every day.

DO JUST ONE THING
Quit multitasking. Single-tasking is far more effective and efficient for productivity.

WRITE A TO-DO LIST
Breaking your day down into managcable tasks is a quick path to clarity, and you get a sense of achievement every time you cross something off! Progress!

TIMING IS EVERYTHING
Work according to your natural biorhythms. Are you a lark or an owl? Go with it, rather than trying to fight it.

ESTABLISH PRIORITIES
Some people like to "eat the frog first"—that is, to get their least-favored task out of the way. However, I find that this can drag you away from doing the most important things. Try doing what's important first.

LISTEN TO YOURSELF
If you're not having the best day, cut yourself some slack. Some days you won't feel well; others, someone else will need you more than you need you. Go with your intuition and take a break when needed, even if that's a break for a whole day.

DELEGATE TASKS
If you can, delegate tasks to others, especially those small but time-consuming tasks, so that you can focus on doing the most important things

SMALL STEPS GO A LONG WAY
Don't judge how much you get done each day in a negative light. Being a perfectionist is only going to harm your productivity.

PRACTICING . . .
overcoming procastination

> "A year from now you will wish you had started today."
> —KAREN LAMB

The task looms over your head like a storm cloud threatening to ruin your day. Fearing just how much you're going to dislike doing the task, you put it off, convincing yourself that you will do it later. We both know you won't, because when "later" comes, your discomfort will be even stronger, making avoidance seem like the only option—until the deadline passes and there are real consequences to face.

As humans, we naturally avoid what's painful. But if we avoided every tiny thing that causes emotional discomfort, then very little would ever get done.

Procrastination usually occurs because of some deep-seated fear. Fears about failure, imperfection, how uncomfortable you expect to feel during a task, or simply not wanting to do a task keep us stuck and unproductive.

What are you procrastinating over right now? Is it something trivial, such as housework or taking your car to the shop? Or is it something major like starting the business you've been dreaming of or having children?

And how much time have you given over to procrastination? How much time has it taken from you? I bet it's not a small amount. And I bet you've had that conversation in your head that goes something like this: "If only I'd started (2 hours/5 weeks/3 years) ago, then I'd have done it by now!"

How are you feeling while you procrastinate? The clients who come to see me over their procrastination do so because procrastinating makes them feel worse. The interesting thing about procrastination is that most of the discomfort we dread about the task is in the dread itself. By the time we get around to completing the task, the pain of anticipating the task has been far worse than what we experience while getting it done.

Don't get me wrong, we all procrastinate at one point or another. It's when procrastination is getting in the way of you living fully, richly, and meaningfully that there is a problem. But what to do about it?

Practicing Overcoming Procrastination

Here's what you can do:

1. Remember that avoiding pain usually gives you more pain. So, if you're avoiding a task, you're likely to feel worse during the avoidance phase than when actually doing it.

2. The hardest part is starting. Once you start, you'll very likely experience a surge in dopamine (the neurochemical in our brains responsible for us feeling motivated), and hopefully you'll want to keep going.

3. Negotiate with yourself. Commit to just five minutes of an activity and then tell yourself that you'll stop. The funny thing is that once you've started, that momentum will very likely keep you going anyway.

4. Ask for help if you need it. Sometimes we stay stuck because we don't know what we need to do next, or how to go about it.

5. Use the Pomodoro Technique for tasks that will take longer than a half hour. Break the task down into periods of 25 minutes of focused attention with a 5-minute break at the end of each productive period. We tend to get more done if we have to focus for only a short burst of time.

6. Remind yourself of your why. Remembering the meaning of a task and how it allows you to live by your values helps!

PRACTICING . . . creativity

> "You can't use up creativity. The more
> you use the more you have."
> —MAYA ANGELOU

Creativity is one of the things that makes us feel most alive. It is the truest expression of ourselves, and it defines the way we interact with the world through our own personal fingerprint. As children, we are naturally creative, and are encouraged to be so. Childhood is driven by the source of creativity—the imagination. We play and paint, dance and draw, sing and tell stories, perhaps all while dressed up as Teenage Mutant Ninja Turtles.

But somewhere in late childhood, we develop the capacity to think analytically and to judge our performance. We become acutely aware of the judgment of others and of the importance of fitting in. Fitting in discourages creativity, because it stifles our spirit with rules. We start to see being vulnerable as risky and choose instead to go for perfect, because perfect seems much safer. Any creative effort we make must be impressive, or else it's a failure.

However, to be perfect in our creativity is almost impossible, leaving vulnerability as the only alternative. And if we can't be vulnerable, then we can't be authentic, leaving us to mask ourselves in a version of creativity that is designed to achieve the approval of the masses, or at least someone important—if we continue being creative at all.

Many people give up on their creativity altogether, which is a crying shame because the possibilities for creativity only increase in adulthood. If we don't continue being creative, we experience adulthood through a flat, one-dimensional lens. And if your creative self is the spirited type, locking them up somewhere between your lungs and your ribs is only going to incense them into constantly reminding you that something is missing. Because it is. Life is bland without creativity.

Shortly, we are going to talk about feeling good enough—an important conversation when it comes to finding your feet with creativity. Please read it, because I'm about to suggest that the only way forward is to shake hands with your creative self again, to rediscover them and spend time with them regularly. But doing so means that you need to get comfortable in your authentic skin and give up the need for approval.

This is no mean feat when we've become so good at doing exactly the opposite. However, creative living is the way to live passionately and richly. It's worth the risk.

Practicing Creativity

Don't wait for the muse to strike you. Here are ways to practice creativity daily.

MEMORY LANE

If it's been a while since you and your creative self were acquainted, think back to the things you loved to do when you were a kid. Did you write poetry? Did you personalize your own clothes? Did you get into Mom's makeup, or draw, or paint, or dance? Whatever your things used to be, don't write them off as belonging to childhood. There is always a way to access that same creative spirit in adulthood, but the hardest part is often remembering what we enjoyed before we locked our creative selves away.

GET CURIOUS

Now is the time to try some things out. Take the things you enjoyed as a child and do them now. Give yourself a chance to immerse yourself in them. And not just the things from childhood—go and try something creative that you've always wanted to do but never tried.

MAKE TIME

The biggest obstacle that most people face is where to fit creativity into their daily lives. For those of us who have dominant creative selves that bang loudly on our insides if we don't let them out, it is absolutely necessary to make time for creativity on a regular basis, not just when we have spare time—because when is that, really? Creativity is not an indulgence, it's essential to well-being. Treat it as such in your priority list!

feeling good enough

"Perfectionism is the voice of the oppressor."
—ANNE LAMOTT

I wish we started conversations about our worth in kindergarten, especially because many of us don't, or didn't, receive these types of messages from our parents, and because childhood's not even over before we are confronted with all the ways in which we can feel not good enough for the rest of our lives.

I've already mentioned our biologically driven desire to fit in, which once protected us from being kicked out of the clan or drawing unwanted attention to our village. And though we're no longer hunter-gatherers, those primordial emotions feel very real. We all know the discomfort of not measuring up and getting rejected (I'm sure just the mention of rejection queues up a slide show of painful memories in your brain). Rejection hurts, and we will do almost anything to avoid it. But what it also does is makes us forget that whether we are doing what everyone else is doing or not, we are still worthy.

I'm not saying you can just give in to your most primitive drives. Causing harm to others is not okay—physically, emotionally, or psychologically. What I'm saying is that the societally accepted measures of worthiness are simply not measures of worthiness.

Here is a list of things that have nothing to do with your self-worth:

• Your weight.
• The label on your shirt.
• The amount in your bank account.
• Where you grew up.
• Where you went to school.
• The number of "likes" you got on your last Instagram post.
• The car you drive.
• Your relationship status.
• Your parental status.
• What you do for a living.
• How much you can lift in the gym.
• Whether or not your eyebrows are on fleek.

Reading this list might make you feel slightly better, but it won't cure your sense of unworthiness. That's why this is all about practice. To change, we have to practice doing the opposite of what we've done in the past—perhaps for the majority of our lives—and focus on the ways in which we are good enough.

Practicing Feeling Good Enough

Because we are genetically wired to feel unworthy, this practice is likely to be lifelong, so beware of any expectations that you may have about doing this for a week and then feeling permanently worthy. Take your time here.

LET GO OF COMPARISON

Use social media mindfully. If it makes you feel worse about yourself, reduce your exposure. This goes for anything you read or watch.

SPEAK OF YOUR OWN VALUE TO YOURSELF

Remind yourself of the true definition of self-worth: that you are worthy, without qualification.

MAKE A MENTAL LIST OF YOUR STRENGTHS

Make a mental list of the things that make you uniquely you. Beware when your mind chatter is being critical for the sake of being critical. Self-criticism is not only painful, it's also a habit. Speak kindly to yourself.Give yourself permission to continue growing, to continue unfolding into yourself, and becoming a better version of what you want to be. And give yourself permission to stay as you are for a while. Nothing blooms all year round.

PRACTICING . . .
forward momentum

"Doing nothing gets you nothing."
—SEAN REICHLE

Wouldn't it be nice if setting a goal meant that we (a) would be motivated to achieve it, (b) would know exactly how to go about it, and (c) would go ahead and take all the steps needed to make it happen?

Some people make it look that easy, but we don't like them all that much, because they make us feel bad about ourselves (just joking . . . kind of). Goals are meaningless unless we do something with them. They are meaningless unless we break them down into steps we can take each day, edging closer to where we want to go. Is the goal specific? Is it meaningful? Is it adaptive? Is it realistic? Is it time-limited? Yes? Then it's time to work out where to start.

But before getting too excited, we need to work out what might get in the way. Prepare for the obstacles and do most of the hard work before they have a chance to stop you in your tracks.

The most common ways you can get blocked are:

1. Forgetting why the goal is important. Keep in touch with your why: Why is this goal meaningful to you? Why will its results benefit your life? Why do you need to pursue this goal, emotionally and personally?

2. Not thinking through exactly what the goal will demand of you. Often things are harder than they sound, and the moment it gets hard, we do what we do best: avoid discomfort and give up. If you want to reach this goal, what will be required of you? Effort? Time? Money? A support crew? Special equipment? New skills, or the polishing of existing skills?

3. Not considering how you will keep going. It's true that starting is the hardest part, but continuing is no walk in the park either. You need to look at what support and rewards you will need to keep you focused along the way. What will you do when it gets hard? When it hurts? When you simply can't be bothered and you want to give up?

Once you've thought through the above for this goal, it's time to break it down into bite-sized, achievable pieces.

Practicing Forward Momentum

Setting a goal is the easy part. Here's how to make every day count toward achieving it.

1. Write down every single step involved in your goal.

2. Order these steps according to priority.

3. Write down all the obstacles that might show up while you're progressing toward your goal and how you might manage them.

4. Write down everything you need to do for the first step, including anything you don't have and/or don't know and will need expert assistance or support with.

5. Take the first step.

6. Review your progress and reassess as you go, adding in any steps that you hadn't considered or that have popped up unexpectedly.

7. Keep going!

PRACTICING . . . breathing

"Feelings come and go like clouds in a windy sky.
Conscious breathing is my anchor."
—THICH NHAT HANH

Sometimes, life steamrolls us and either flattens us under its demands or leaves us scrambling to outrun it. Perhaps it's that your schedule is a constant game of *Tetris*. Perhaps your most recent path has been particularly unforgiving in the number of crises it presented to you all at once. Whatever it is for you, I'll bet that it's unimaginably heavy, this load of yours, and that you're exhausted from trying to carry it, get out from underneath it, or run from it as far as your legs will take you

Stress and anxiety are drivers for action. In the right amounts, they improve your performance, focus your attention, and give you the energy to Get. It. Done. Too much stress or anxiety will do the opposite. It will leave you pacing around the kitchen table, not realizing that your sunglasses are already on your head. They will warp your concentration, deplete your energy, and cause you to be busy but unproductive, or stuck in a catatonic state in front of your inbox. Either way, your energy expenditure will likely be spent on racing around, trying to get a sense that you're making headway.

When stress and anxiety gets to be too much, we lose the capacity to deal effectively with the demands in front of us and instead seek to simply survive. This usually means one of two things: we fight or we flee. Both alternatives cause us to lose contact with the here and now in favor of worrying about what's to come, or what's already happened. Perhaps you've run out of fight and you're sick of the effort to keep up, or outrun it all, externally, internally, or both.

The answer is in your breath. Your breath is your one constant: always with you and always available as an anchor when you come untethered. Come back to your breath to help you focus, slow down, and gather yourself, rather than flailing around for the sake of expelling your anxiety.

We can't be ahead of it all, all the time. We can't expect that our thoughts and feelings won't get the better of us every now and again and leave us in a hope deficit or in a worry surplus. Returning to the breath allows us to return to a neutral place. Even for just one of the 1,440 minutes of each day, returning to the breath allows us to come back to center, catch up, perhaps even stop completely. It is a chance to reset, to start the day again. And who doesn't want that? Who doesn't *need* that, every now and again? I know I do. And the beauty is that no one needs to know anything about it. No one needs to know about your 60-second oxygenated vacation away from Tuesday, or Wednesday night, or Monday morning.

Practicing Breathing

Here's a simple and useful process for reconnecting with your breathing.

VISUALIZE YOUR BREATH AS A CYCLE:

1.

Inhale for 4 seconds

2.

Hold for 4 seconds

3.

Exhale for 4 seconds

4.

Hold for 4 seconds

Repeat for a minute or two. If 4 seconds feels too long, shorten to 3 seconds.

Use this technique whenever you need to
find an anchor in the present moment.

PRACTICING . . .
a positive inner voice

> "You're only as good as your next
> thought of yourself."
> —CURTIS TYRONE JONES

If you are going to practice only one habit from this book to improve your sense of self-worth, I strongly encourage you to choose this one. Your inner monologue matters.

Imagine that I was yelling at you for every one of your waking hours today. Now imagine that I was doing that all week. And now for the whole of this month. What about for the past decade? Or since you became old enough to ever feel like you aren't worthy? Feels pretty overwhelming, right?

Perhaps you're reading this book because this is what you've experienced, except the criticism and badgering and condemnation has not come from me. It has come from you, to you. For all that time.

If someone in your life treated you that way, for the majority of your life, you might very well end up psychologically damaged because of it. There's only so much we can withstand before there is significant healing to be done. And it's the same for the way we treat ourselves. If you treat yourself like that for all the years that it's possible to be aware of measuring up to some standard of enough, you'll injure your heart. You may eventually not like yourself much anymore, if at all.

Sometimes the internal chatter doesn't start as internal. Maybe your inner voice reflects the external messages you received and mimics those of a critical parent, or a teacher who told you that you would never amount to anything, or a partner who pointed out all your flaws. The point is that the only way we address those voices is by consciously becoming aware of when we talk to ourselves in a destructive way.

The way we treat ourselves affects the quality of our lives overall, not to mention our relationships with others, and of course, our sense of worthiness and value as a human being. For too many of us, the enemy lines are drawn and we habitually attack from within.

What if there was another way? What if you just started speaking kindly to yourself?

Be careful of excuses showing up at this point. Yes, it's easier said than done. But the effort involved in speaking kindly to yourself is well worth it. I'm not trying to sell you a revolutionary idea here. All I'm doing is inviting you to try it and notice the difference for yourself. You have the choice to befriend yourself or continue the war.

Practicing a Positive Inner Voice

Don't beat yourself up; instead, try the following to practice speaking kindly to yourself.

BRING IT

Bring the willingness. Bring the effort. Bring the acceptance that you won't get it right every time. Bring the attitude that this is a practice and that it's worth doing because you are worth it. Bring your attention—when you lapse back into a default critical voice, notice it and start again.

START A CONVERSATION

Start a new conversation with yourself. Where you usually speak about your weaknesses, mistakes, defects, and all the ways in which you have gone wrong and may go wrong in the future, try doing it differently. Start a conversation where you try encouraging yourself. Where you speak to your strengths, forgive yourself, go easy on yourself, and remind yourself of what you're capable of. Have a conversation where you acknowledge what you're doing well.

WATCH YOUR TONE AND LANGUAGE

Be mindful of your tone. Choose gentle words. Lose the labels, judgments, and expectations. Speak from a voice that you'd like to be friends with.

PRACTICE

Practice every day. Start again when you need to. Give yourself permission to be learning and trying and doing things differently.

setting boundaries

'No' is a complete sentence."
—ANNE LAMOTT

A boundary is something that indicates a limit, and personal boundaries are the fundamental, often intangible limits we're interested in for happiness and well-being. Because if you don't set boundaries for yourself, who will?

I ask because I see too many people hurt when their boundaries are crossed, but surprised that they had a hand in the violation in the first place by leaving their emotional gates open.

An emotional gate is the barrier we all must draw around ourselves to preserve our energy; time; and emotional, physical, and psychological resources. Without these barriers, we have no way of conserving our personal resources. Instead, we give them away. Maybe not willingly, but there are those around us who are highly attuned to seeking out available reserves in others—even when they are not offered explicitly.

And what do I mean about having a hand in the violation that occurs when your boundaries are crossed? Well, if you don't close the gate, please don't be surprised when someone walks through it. If there's nothing to stop people, not everyone will stop themselves. We could get all high and mighty and say that others should act respectfully and responsibly so as not to cross your boundaries. But what if they don't know (or care) where the line is? What if *you* don't even know where the line is?

To set effective boundaries, we must know where our boundaries are. Sometimes, you'll only know a boundary exists when it's been crossed. Those are painful lessons we never forget. Once you know where your lines are, it's up to you to enforce them.

This is where many people struggle, often feeling selfish or guilty if they insist on a boundary being observed by others. Setting boundaries is not being selfish—It is the ultimate form of self-respect, and self-respect is paramount for self-worth (and therefore, for happiness and well-being). Boundaries act as pillars in effective communication with others by clearly defining what you will and won't do. They help others hold realistic expectations of you and what you have to give, and help them operate in a manner that is respectful.

This is also a process of getting to know yourself. The things you accepted in your twenties may not be the same things you'd accept in your thirties or forties. Only you know where your limits are, and it's your responsibility to communicate them to those around you. It doesn't make sense to be upset at people for crossing a boundary that they didn't know was there in the first place, especially if you've habitually let them cross that line in the past and never told them otherwise.

Practicing Setting Boundaries

Here are some ways to help you draw the line when it's needed.

LEARN ABOUT YOURSELF

Get to know where your boundaries are. Think of the time, energy, and personal resources you have that are available to others. Anything that you need to sustain you needs to stay with you.

DRAW THE LINE

Drawing the line means that you respect that your boundary is there. Once you've set your boundaries, be prepared to communicate to others where your lines are. You can't expect other people to respect your boundaries if you don't.

ASSERTIVELY DEFEND YOUR LINE

Once the line is there, you need to enforce it, because if you don't, then who will? This might mean upsetting some people, or letting go of some people in your circle. It might mean that you learn a new language, beginning with the word "no."

LET GO OF PEOPLE PLEASING

Let's be real here: Some people will misinterpret your request to respect a boundary as rudeness or selfishness. These people are usually either unable to set their own boundaries, or they're used to walking all over everyone for their own gain and are disappointed that you won't let them do the same. Either way, you need to uphold your boundaries for your own mental health.

SPEAK THE LANGUAGE OF SELF-RESPECT

Practice saying no. Over and over again. Practice saying no without justification. Practice saying no as a full sentence. Practice saying no simply because it's the right thing for you at the time.

PRACTICING . . .

getting perspective

> "We don't see things as they are,
> we see them as we are."
> —ANAÏS NIN

We humans behave with a suite of beliefs, judgments, memories, and thoughts that inform our way of seeing the world. And each day, there's the possibility that something will occur, or someone will cross our path, that challenges our expectations about how the world should be. These "rules" that we have about ourselves, others, and the world at large are useful for processing the millions of pieces of information that we receive while we are awake. They help us categorize and make meaning of our lives.

But sometimes, these rules are blinkers. They stop us from seeing a bigger picture. We get locked into our expectations and respond rigidly when those expectations are violated. Sometimes our perspective can also be blinkered by our emotional state. Stress and anxiety can cause our view to narrow so that we see only the negative aspects of a difficult situation.

When life doesn't go our way, we need a means of opening up, of overcoming the blind spots and considering another point of view. This is known as perspective-taking.

Think of the things you already do to get perspective. When

you feel overwhelmed, or angry, or resentful, how do you move through your feelings to see the situation in a way that no longer keeps you stuck? Maybe your current strategies work, like talking to a trusted friend or focusing on gratitude. Or maybe they don't, like ruminating, or overdosing on caffeine, or lashing out at someone close.

I'm not here with a failure-proof set of guidelines for perspective-taking, unfortunately. I'm here with some suggestions that I've seen work. We generally need perspective when we are feeling shaky. When the world doesn't look as we think it should, it's a vulnerable time. Go gently with yourself and take these suggestions where you feel like they fit.

Practicing Getting Perspective

Losing perspective happens to everyone. Here's how to keep yourself on track.

NOTICE WHEN YOU'VE LOST PERSPECTIVE

Recognize those situations in which you lose perspective. What are your warning signs? Do you make rash decisions that don't fit with your values? Do you become antagonistic? Do you push people away? It's important to be gentle rather than judgmental with yourself. It's equally important to be honest.

ACKNOWLEDGE THE DISCOMFORT

When you're in that space, perhaps feeling like you have lost your anchor, acknowledge the discomfort. Just don't let it dictate your actions.

ASK QUESTIONS

Ask yourself some helpful questions to gain perspective:

- What can I control here? What is outside of my control?
- Will worrying about the situation help me change it or feel better about it?
- Will this matter tomorrow? Next week? Next month? Next year?
- How could I see the situation differently?

FIND PERSPECTIVE WITH ACTIONS

Here are some other things you can do to gain perspective:

- Seek out someone you trust and run the situation by them. Get another point of view.
- Remind yourself of everything you are grateful for.
- Ensure you are eating well and hydrating. Brain chemistry changes according to your diet which then affects your mental state.

MAKING SPACE FOR. . .

imperfection
crises
your own journey
holding pain lightly
big decisions
intuition
hope
forgiveness

Let's be real here: The world is not perfect. It makes no promises about always going our way, and owes us nothing just because we were born. As such, we need to make space for life getting hard. It will, but we will survive it, and we can thrive through the hard times if we work on building our resilience muscles. To do so, we need to be flexible. We need to understand that we can fall, but we can catch ourselves too.

This section is about how we make space for the challenging stuff, because challenges are more easily embraced when we have space to step back and observe them. It's about the stuff we aren't taught at school, the stuff we wish our parents had taught us but didn't, and the stuff that we often reach adulthood without truly understanding: how to forgive, how to stop tripping ourselves up in the pursuit for perfection, how to make big decisions, and how to love ourselves unconditionally.

Obviously, this list is not exhaustive. It doesn't cover every aspect of living meaningfully. But what it does cover are the things that we all struggle with at some stage, the things that cause us to run when we should stay, to fight when we should make peace, and to loathe ourselves and others when we should turn to toward kindness.

MAKING SPACE FOR . . .
imperfection

"To banish imperfection is to destroy expression, to check exertion, to paralyze vitality."
—JOHN RUSKIN

Perfection is a coach with a chip on his shoulder. No matter how hard you work, he sits there blowing his whistle, telling you to do it again. Get it right. Make it perfect. He threatens you with embarrassment if you don't follow orders. Sometimes, he promises a break and a nice long rest, as long as you can prove that you make the grade. And by the way, the grade is 100% all the time, with no special consideration clause or exceptions recognized for prior learning.

But perfection doesn't only have demands. It also has a list of performance benchmarks that it will gleefully point out that you're not meeting. All the ways in which you are not good enough and don't measure up make a colorful bullet-point list. You don't think perfection will let you get away with thinking that you did all right, do you? Because you'd be sorely mistaken if you thought that was the case.

Perfection is a time waster. It paralyzes you through procrastination, self-criticism, and fear of failure. Think about all that perfection has robbed you of. Time? Money? Self-esteem? Definitely energy, right? Maybe it's robbed you of relationships, especially the relationship you have with yourself. And maybe it's constantly dragged you out of the present moment and kept you in your head, panicking about all the ways you've failed in the past and how you will prevent them from happening in the future.

Some people allow perfection to convince them that it has special powers that will help them reach their potential. They believe that if they stop striving for perfection the Gods of Enough will reject them as failures. Perhaps they don't believe exactly that, but they believe they won't be the best version of themselves if they lower the bar—as if the only other option is "below mediocre."

I don't know about you, but this just doesn't fit with what I know to be true, neither in myself or in my clients. People who are perfectionistic are not motivated by reaching a state of perfection. Maybe only about 5% of their striving is about that. The other 95% is about the promises that perfection makes. They are motivated by the fact that perfection promises to have them be the best, to belong to the cool group, and to be stamped with approval as being worthy.

In my experience, the rigid and derisive nature of perfectionism doesn't contribute positively to well-being. In fact, it's damaging to self-worth. Letting go of perfectionism requires us to change. When befriending ourselves is our foundation, the possibilities for growth are wider, richer, and happier.

Making Space for Imperfection

Perfection is a myth. Here are some ways to find the space for your natural imperfections.

PERMISSION TO TRY

Give yourself permission to try. Without permission, I guarantee that perfection will either burn you out so you have to stop anyway or have you paralyzed on the starting block for a very long time.

TAKE AN ATTITUDE OF PROGRESS

Go for progress. Go for being part of the process. It's this attitude that allows you to acknowledge every part of you that is trying.

THINK OF PERFECTION AS AN ILLUSION

Because that's what it is, unless you're an android— and you're not, right?

ASK THE HARD QUESTIONS

Has perfection ever brought you the result you were seeking? What promises are perfection making that you know to be false? What is everyone else chasing that you think they have but you don't? What has perfection convinced you to believe about your own self-worth?

MAKING SPACE FOR . . . crises

> "I think when tragedy occurs, it presents a choice. You can give in to the void: the emptiness that fills your heart, your lungs, constricts your ability to think or even breathe. Or you can try to find meaning."
> —SHERYL SANDBERG

I wish I could say that if you did all the right things and you were simply a good person, life would reward you accordingly with a smooth path and good weather. Although this wish is the stuff of rainbows and unicorns, our brains do have a way of unfairly cushioning the task of living with uncertainty, injustice, and tragedy in the world. You see, to live comfortably, humans make cognitive assumptions to ease their sense of threat. These assumptions include:

- The world is a safe and predictable place.
- Good things happen to good people, and bad things happen to bad people.
- Bad things are more likely to happen to others than to me. Overall, I am a good person.

These assumptions help us to feel safer while going about our daily lives, but they aren't always accurate—obviously—because the very nature of a crisis is that it's unexpected. It violates these assumptions and compromises our physical and/or psychological safety. It makes us question our footing and place in difficult and tragic things. It reminds us that sometimes life will happen to us, and we need to find a way to cope.

Even though crises are going to occur, I'm not actually suggesting that we prepare for them. I'm not suggesting that we live in a future that's going to be disastrous, like people with post-traumatic stress disorder often do. Instead, I'm suggesting that we accept that life isn't always the way we'd like it to be, and that when crises show up, we make space for them without fighting or flailing out against the experience and making it worse.

It's what we do with our circumstances that defines us, not the circumstances themselves. It's about knowing that our circumstances are not our identity and that we are strong enough to cope. It's a process of backing yourself and your decisions, rather than imagining what you could have done differently. How we approach what we can and can't control determines our experience.

It's worth noting that we can't always know the duration or intensity of a crisis. Some crises, such as a fender bender, are over in a day and require a sprintlike approach to coping and problem-solving. Others are long term and require marathon effort and energy, such as caring for a loved one with a terminal illness. A crisis might demand more energy from you at different stages. The start might look different from the middle and the end might be followed by an aftermath. But hopefully, you can make enough room in your life to deal with this mess without uprooting your identity or peace of mind.

Making Space
for Crises

This can't happen, you say. But a crisis can, and it might. Here's how to make room for it.

LOOK AFTER YOURSELF

Take a breath. Take time out when you can. Return to the basics of eating, sleeping, and taking care of yourself as well as possible.

ALLOW YOUR EXPERIENCE TO BE WHAT IT IS

Don't judge your experience. Don't force it to be something other than what it is, and don't try to avoid or deny the fact that it's happening.

REACH OUT

We can't always think clearly in a crisis, and help from someone we trust can bring some perspective. Seek support if you need it. Expecting to survive a crisis alone puts unnecessary pressure on yourself.

TAKE ACTION

Especially in the case of a long-term crisis, give yourself a break from working towards your major life goals. Instead, focus on the next step that you need to take to be effective in the present moment. Sometimes that's doing the thing that will help you tread water, rather than sink. And sometimes, that's the thing that will help you to swim forward.

MAKING SPACE FOR . . .
your own journey

"There ain't no journey what
don't change you some."
—DAVID MITCHELL

Sometimes, we care far too much about things that don't help us grow, improve, or feel good about ourselves. In fact, sometimes we care about things that actively work against maintenance of our self-worth, and those things usually involve comparing ourselves to other people.

Comparison starts early, especially if you have brothers or sisters. And if you don't have siblings, you'll soon end up comparing yourself to people on math quizzes, at dance or soccer practice, and through the veritable minefield that is puberty. Then there are social media feeds and the quest to gain approval on the career ladder.

When we care too much about other people and their opinions and judgments of us (which we are quick to assume are negative, usually without legitimate evidence), it's a recipe for inner turmoil and feelings of self-reproach. Comparison habitually places our focus on the wrong place: on things and people outside of our control and away from our own journey. And it can go either way—you might find yourself seeking approval from someone important to you, or taking pleasure in considering yourself superior to someone who you believe is not doing as well as you. Both comparisons are weak scaffolds for well-being and healthy relationships.

In other words, comparison is always unfair. It doesn't honor the unique path of your own journey or that of the person you're comparing yourself to. And how long will you be in a holding pattern before you start living the life you truly want to live if you have to wait until you have evidence that everyone in your life likes you and approves of your every decision?

Again, I'm not saying that this is easy. How do we ignore our caveman wiring for seeking approval? Well, we don't. But being aware of it means we're less likely to be incapacitated by it. Awareness allows you to remember that even though comparison is inevitable, you can make space to be gentle with yourself, carry negative thoughts lightly, and remind yourself to go at your pace, in a direction that's right for you today.

Making Space for Your Own Journey

No one else can walk your path for you. Here are some ways to make room for your own journey.

NOTICE COMPARISON

The problem is not that we are wired to compare; the problem is when we do so without awareness. Notice the comparison and choose how you carry it, if you carry it at all.

LEARN ABOUT YOURSELF

Get to know yourself. Get to know what progress looks like for you. The more you can see it, the more you can . . .

ACKNOWLEDGE HOW FAR YOU'VE COME

Celebrate your progress regularly. If you constantly point out how far you've got to go, you'll never stop to appreciate where you are.

MAKE THE JOURNEY EASIER

Change your expectations, speak kindly to yourself, reduce exposure to things that make the journey harder than it needs to be (such as social media or spending time with people who build themselves up and put you down).

CONNECT WITH YOUR VALUES

Choose the type of person you want to be and what you want to stand for. Do you want to be the type that tears another down to feel good about yourself?

FIND GRATITUDE

Be grateful for your own efforts, lessons, and achievements on the way. Gratitude is the strongest antidote we have to feelings of unworthiness.

holding pain lightly

"The best way out is always through."
—ROBERT FROST

Beyond the instinct to simply survive, the strongest human instinct we possess is to avoid pain. But if we attempt to live a life without any pain at all, then we make no place for processing tough emotions, or for striving to achieve things, or for simply being resilient to the discomfort that occurs as part of the natural flow of existence. If you fight off emotional discomfort, you only end up feeding the pain and encouraging it to overwhelm you. Running from it, denying it, or trying to cover up or smother it is a recipe for prolonging and intensifying the pain.

What if there is another way? What if I told you that you could do pain differently? I'm sure your interest is piqued here, but I can guarantee that the answer probably isn't what you expect, because it's counterintuitive to our natural approach to things that hurt us. The bad news is, I don't have any secret method of exorcising your pain for you. The good news is that this technique is powerful and effective, even if it won't turn your pain off.

The most effective thing you can do in the face of pain is to accept it. I do not mean you have to like your negative emotions, or want them, or enjoy them. Instead, I mean acknowledging and accepting the presence of pain as part of your experience, without judgment or struggle.

At first, it may seem impossible. I mean, who really wants to accept pain? Isn't that just an invitation for the pain to have full control over you? Well, surprisingly not. Accepting pain is very different from wallowing in pain. While wallowing in pain is about resistance, helplessness, and a sense of being consumed by it, accepting pain is the opposite. It is about making a conscious choice to drop the struggle with the pain and sit with it in the moment, without letting it drive your choices. By accepting pain, we free up our energy to decide what to do next, even if that's just in the next minute.

Acceptance frees us from being bound to the pain. It allows us to move through the pain to process it and reach the other side.

Making Space for Holding Pain Lightly

With these steps, you'll have room to embrace and accept your pain without wallowing in it.

DESCRIBE THE FEELING AS IF IT WERE AN OBJECT INSIDE YOU

What shape does it have? Where is it in your body? How much space is it taking up? Does it have a temperature? What texture does it have? Does it have a weight? Does it have a color? Is it moving or is it still? Is it causing any pressure anywhere?

BREATHE AROUND IT

Use your breath to imagine opening up. If the feeling is in your chest or your belly, you can use your breath to feel your chest or belly expand. If the feeling is somewhere else in your body, follow your breath and with each inhalation visualize the place in your body expanding around the feeling to give it space.

DON'T TRY TO CHANGE THE FEELING

We are not trying to numb ourselves here. We are simply allowing the feeling to be what it is without forcing it, or trying to get rid of it, or changing it into something more pleasant.

DISCLAIMER

This technique will often result in you feeling less overwhelmed by the emotion. Sometimes this technique is a container, sometimes it's a diffuser. It's worth remembering that sometimes your mind will try to talk you out of doing anything to help yourself. Step back from those thoughts. Your mind doesn't drive the bus, your actions do.

MAKING SPACE FOR . . .
big decisions

"Your life changes the moment you make a new, congruent, and committed decision."
—TONY ROBBINS

You know those times when you're facing a crossroads? I'm not talking about what you're going to have for lunch today. Although that's an important decision, it's not exactly a big one. I'm talking about the decisions that show up in life that require pondering, research, analysis, input from others, and guidance from your intuition. The decisions in which taking either fork in the road are fraught with big emotions. These decisions can scare you, or hurt your heart, or bring up guilt, or make you wonder whether you can trust hope, or simply cause you to feel confused and anxious because you can't know what will happen in the future.

Only you can assess the gravity of the decision for yourself. Obviously, if it's bringing up discomfort for you, it's important to you and deserves your attention. But how do you go about giving it your attention? What's the process you should use to work out which way to go next? Well, first, I want to talk about the pressure we place on ourselves to make the right decision. The truth is that in many situations, we can't possibly know what the right decision is, because we are not fortune-tellers. I can't tell you if you should have a baby when you're undecided.

I can't tell you if you should quit your job to start your business right now. I can't tell you if you should get married, or divorce your husband ten years after saying your vows. But what I can encourage you to do is listen to your own wisdom: what you know about what truly matters to you, what you know about the things you've done well in the past, the lessons you've learned from your mistakes and failures, and, importantly, what you know from the intuitive inner voice calling for your attention.

Sometimes, the emotions that arise at a crossroads are so consuming that you may feel the urge to shut down and put the choice off. Be mindful of avoidance, though. Sometimes we convince ourselves that we don't know which direction to head in when we don't want to acknowledge something hard or confrontational. Take your values, your lessons, your strengths, and your intuition and face your decision. We can't solve a problem and make a choice without facing what's in front of us head on.

Making Space for Big Decisions

Big decisions can be paralyzing. These tips will help you make space for them and move forward.

DO YOUR RESEARCH

Give yourself a limited period of time to research your decision. If you don't have time to do research, talk to people you trust about their experiences in similar situations.

LIST THE PROS AND CONS

Use the table provided on the opposite page to make a list of pros and cons. Rate each one in terms of its importance (1 point for not as important, 2 points for moderately important,and 3 points for very important). Add up the scores in each column. Use the final scores as information only, not a definitive answer.

CONSIDER LESSONS FROM THE PAST

Consider what you already know about your strengths, problems you've solved well, and decisions that have worked out previously.

CONNECT WITH YOUR VALUES

Connect with your values. What matters deep down inside your heart? Who do you want to be? What do you want to stand for?

USE YOUR INTUITION

What is your inner voice saying? Listen to yourself. You know more than you think you do.

TAKE ACTION

You won't always be ready to take action. You might still feel confused, or overwhelmed. But the only way to to know how something is going to work out, is to try it. Take the first step; once you do, courage will show up.

Making Space for Big Decisions

List and rate your pros and cons below.

PROS

....
....
....
....
....
....
....
....
....
....
....
....

CONS

....
....
....
....
....
....
....
....
....
....
....
....

FINAL SCORE: ....

FINAL SCORE: ....

MAKING SPACE FOR . . .
intuition

"I believe in intuitions and inspirations . . . I sometimes feel that I am right. I do not know that I am."
—ALBERT EINSTEIN

How often do you stop and take the time to listen to what your inner voice has to say? That voice is very easily drowned out by the voices of those close to you, the voices of the critics in your head, people whose approval you are seeking, people you admire (even if you don't know them personally), and messages you receive from the media and the culture around you. It's easy to think that your voice has gone quiet, but it's likely you just can't hear it over the din of the external noise of daily life.

Life without guidance from your intuition is akin to a toy boat crossing an ocean, at the mercy of the current and weather around it, without an anchor or internal structures to help hold it upright. Your intuition is that anchor. It is the thing that you can always trust will be there when you need grounding, direction, and reassurance.

I see two common struggles when it comes to people's intuition. First, people underestimate its power. And second, they have made a mistake in the past and no longer trust what their intuition has to say. To this I would say that your intuition is the most powerful voice in your life. It's the key to living authentically and in alignment with your core values. When we make mistakes, they are never solely about the fact that we listened to our intuition. Mistakes are always about a collection of tiny events, choices, and pieces of information that we put together in a moment in time to respond to the world, to other people, or to ourselves, which ultimately doesn't take our lives in a direction that we want to go. It's never the result of just one thing.

What if you were to listen to your inner voice and really hear what it has to say? What if you were to offer it a place in your approach to living? What if it helped you make decisions, connect with your values, and guide your actions?

That's all well and good, but how do you connect with your intuition if you can't remember what it sounds like? To harness its power, you need to make space where it can be heard, and where you can accept it.

Let go.

Making Space for Intuition

Your intuition is there—it just needs room to move. Try these methods to give it space.

GET QUIET

By quiet, I don't necessarily mean that you need to sit in silence (although this can help greatly), I mean quiet from the "noise" generated by the other voices inside you. Specifically, watch out for critical voices, scared voices, and voices that are out to sabotage you.

CANCEL OUT EXTERNAL NOISE

Let go of the opinions and judgments of others. Let go of any negativity hovering around you. Let go of any pressure you feel from the media, social feeds, or parental/authoritative influences around you.

LISTEN

Listen with patience. You may not hear it immediately, but over time that voice will become louder and will have a clarity you can't ignore. Listen with intention. What will you do about what that voice is saying? What keeps coming up? What are you trying not to hear? What are you trying to force it to say? If you completely let go and let it speak of its own accord, what is your intuition telling you?

MAKING SPACE FOR . . .
hope

"Hope is the thing with feathers
That perches in the soul,
And sings the tune without the words,
And never stops at all."
—EMILY DICKINSON

Hope is both a feeling and a skill. It's fuel for motivation and a balm for sadness and anxiety. You might be able to pretend to be happy, or pretend to be optimistic, but it's pretty much impossible to pretend to be hopeful. Making hope a habit is like installing a sensor light that's triggered when darkness falls. And the beauty is that you can learn to be hopeful. You can practice being hopeful. You just need to make space for it.

You don't need to feel positive to be hopeful. In fact, you could be going through an extremely difficult time in your life with a barrage of painful feelings and still feel hopeful. You see, hope is not about putting on rose-colored glasses. It's about acknowledging your personal agency to be able to effect change when you want to. Hope acknowledges your strengths and capacity to cope when things get difficult. It connects you with the things that make life worthwhile, even when you're relying on a flicker of light in the darkness.

Don't get me wrong, it's common to have times when you feel hopeless. Everyone has moments where life becomes cloudy and we can't see where we are going or remember the point of it all. Most of the time, these moments are brief. If you've been feeling like this for more than a couple of weeks, now is the time to reach out to someone close to you and let them know how you are feeling. Hope doesn't always have to come from within. Sometimes, it arrives in the palm of a helping hand—that of a doctor, teacher, or friend.

When you learn how to turn the light of hope on for yourself, you can withstand anything life throws at you. This is even the case if you're not a naturally optimistic person. Like any habit for happiness, all you need is a little bit of willingness, a regular commitment to practice, and the right techniques—which is why you're here, reading this book!

Making Space for Hope

You always have hope . . . try these exercises to make the space for it.

GET SOME PERSPECTIVE

When you look backwards look for lessons. When you look around, look for reality, and not your mind's interpretation of reality. When you look forward, look for possibilities.

BE PERSISTENT

Find your backbone. Hope requires you to show up time and again. It is resilience in action, and to be resilient means you do everything you need to do to be able to say you coped effectively with the situation. It means you ask for help if you need to, and you may even rest for a time. But you resist the urge to give up.

MAKE PROGRESS

Hope is an action-taker. You can't just sit on the sidelines, assuming that life will turn around for you. But if you'd like things to change in the direction of life that sparks your soul, you need to take action to make that happen. That action might be difficult, and perhaps it won't work out perfectly. But without action, hope has no momentum with which to move forward.

HAVE FAITH

Have faith that things will work out. Have faith in yourself. Have faith in a higher power. Have faith in the universe. It doesn't matter what it is, but if you have faith, this gives you somewhere to place your trust in times of uncertainty.

MAKING SPACE FOR . . .
forgiveness

"Forgiveness does not change the past,
but it does enlarge the future."
—PAUL BOESE

I think deep down we are all seeking happiness, but the key to happiness is not the pleasant feelings themselves. It's the experience of inner peace.

Okay, you're unlikely to find a permanent state of peacefulness, and that's not what I'm suggesting. Instead, this is about finding different gateways to psychological freedom, and one of those gateways that promises more freedom than you will ever find without it is forgiveness. Before your mind has a chance to land on the person or situation that has hurt you most, I want to start with you, because when I talk about forgiveness, you must start within first. If you can't forgive yourself, you will never truly understand the peace that is available to you. Mistakes. Poor decisions. Lapses in judgment. Habits that have harmed you. Hurt you've caused in others. Ways you've betrayed yourself. We've all got a laundry list of regrets that threaten to keep us prisoner in our heads and hearts. Self-forgiveness is the process of reminding yourself of your humanity, frailties and all. Without making excuses for or approving of your past actions, you can acknowledge that you are not perfect. You can seek forgiveness from others while you come to a place where you can forgive yourself, understanding that one is not dependent on the other.

Making space for forgiveness requires us to acknowledge that personal evolution is fraught with misdemeanors based on what we can't know before we know it. Forgiveness frees us to be human, to be sorry, to offer apologies to others and ourselves, to seek to rectify our mistakes where possible, and to move on with the intention of doing better next time.

Offering forgiveness to others is often just as difficult as forgiving ourselves. Sometimes we want to hold onto resentment and hurt as evidence of the gross psychological, physical, and/or emotional injury caused by the other person. And the truth is, there may never be adequate justice, considering that the system of law by which we are governed is far from perfect. I speak about forgiveness while acknowledging the deep scars that many of us have, which burn and ache long after the event. I'm definitely not going to tell you that you need to forgive anyone or anything. You don't *have to* do anything. But what I will suggest is that forgiveness is your way through the pain. It won't fix the pain. But it will relieve you of having to carry the burden of resentment and revenge and anger on top of the pain.

Making Space for Forgiveness

Here are some ways to allow yourself enough room to forgive.

FORGIVE YOURSELF FOR NOT WANTING TO FORGIVE

Coming to a place where you are ready to forgive takes space and perhaps some mental gymnastics. Give yourself permission to get there in your own time.

COMMIT TO PRACTICING LETTING GO

Bring willingness. Bring openness. Commit to yourself that you'll practice letting go of the hurt caused and the person who caused it, even if it's for thirty seconds each day. You don't have to forget what someone did, but you can let go of what it caused for you and instead, bring your focus back to your own healing.

FOCUS ON HEALING

Focus on your own healing, rather than on getting revenge for the wounds in the first place. Your healing is something that you have control over and can take responsibility for.

ALLOW FORGIVENESS TO BE A PROCESS

Maybe you can't imagine a time when you will completely forgive. Allow it to be a process that you practice indefinitely, if needs be.

CONCLUDING WISHES

It is my hope that this book has added value to your daily life. We all deserve to thrive.

As I'm sure you've noticed, I passionate about many points here. This isn't my attempt at playing drill sergeant, barking orders at you about relationships, self-awareness, and well-being. Instead, I'm simply making sure we are clear about the cards on the table here: forming habits for happiness takes effort and goes beyond just feeling good.

It's about breaking your routine and making an effort, every day, to be the person you want to be.

May you prioritize your well-being, because your life depends on it! Don't settle for merely existing when you can grow, thrive, and be happy. I know you can do this!